The *Ultimate Little*
MARTINI BOOK

by
Ra

D0963798

OVER 1000 MARTINI RECIPES

*Cover design by Tim Williams, Tim Williams Illustrations,
Cumming, GA, (770) 888-6419; FAX: (770) 888-6407;
E-mail: twillustration@mindspring.com*

Inside cartoons by Bob Schochet, Highland Mills, NY

Edited by Jaclyn Wilson Foley and Loretta Natiello

Printed in the United States of America

First printing July 2000
10 9 8 7 6 5 4 3 2 1

© Copyright 2000 by Raymond P. Foley
Published by FOLEY Publishing

ISBN # 0-9617655-7-7

Foley Publishing Corp.

DEDICATION

*This book is dedicated to all the
martini drinkers and bartenders
who stir, shake and serve.
Also to Jaclyn Marie and Ryan Foley
and the rest of the tribe!*

ACKNOWLEDGMENT

Allied Domecq Spirits USA

Angostura International Ltd.

Anheuser-Busch, Inc., Diane Burnell

Austin, Nichols & Co., Inc

Bacardi USA, Inc.

Banta Book Group, Bob Christopher

Barton Incorporated

Branca Products Corporation

Brown-Forman Beverages Worldwide

Cairns & Associates, Inc.

Charles Jacquin et Cie., Inc, Patricia Bornmann

John Cooper, Kevin O'Brien

Coco Lopéz, Inc, Jose Suarez, R. Jake Jacobsen

Crillon Importers

Dozortsev & Sons Enterprises, Ltd.

Dunwoodie Communications, Greg Cohen

Finlandia Vodka Americas, Inc.

Heaven Hill Distilleries, Inc.

Jim Beam Brands Worldwide, Inc.

Kobrand Corp.

Kratz & Jensen, Inc., Christine Deussen, Alicia DiFolco

Major Peters Bloody Mary Mix

Manitowoc Ice, Inc., Larry Hagman

Marie Brizard Wines and Spirits, USA

Miller Brewing Company, Joan Zitzke

Mott's USA, Jeff Polisoto
National Cherry Board, Cheryl Kroupa
Niche Marketing
Remy Amerique, Robert Rentsch
Schieffelin & Somerset, Jeff Pogash
Seagram North America, Robert Dubin, Arthur Shapiro
Skyy Spirits LLC
Robert Suffredini
Steve Baron Communications
The Baddish Group, Laura Baddish
The Food Group, Mark Bloom
The Gang at Maker's Mark
Todhunter International, Inc.
Top Shelf Marketing, George and Kelly Borrello
UDV North America
Vita Mix
Waring Products, Joan Gioiella

Special thanks to Jimmy Zazzali, Matt Wojciak,
John Cowan, Michael Cammarano, Charles Chop,
Marvin Solomon, the Rinaldis (Millie and Anthony),
plus Loretta Natiello, Julie Wilson Christopher and
Erica DeWitte for putting this to paper.

Also, to all those who submitted recipes to
WWW.BARTENDER.COM and the readers of
BARTENDER Magazine.

A SHORT HISTORY OF THE ORIGINS OF THE MARTINI

1. By Bartender Professor Jerry Thomas of San Francisco from a stranger on his way to Martinez. Made with Gin, Vermouth, Bitters, Dash of Maraschino.

2. By a Bartender in Martinez, California, for a gold miner who struck it rich. The miner ordered champagne for the house. But there was none. The Bartender offered something better, a "Martinez Special," some (Sauterne) and Gin. The rich miner spread the word ordering throughout California a "Martinez Special."

3. After the British army rifle: The Martini and Henry. The rifle was known for its kick, like the first sip of Gin and "it" ("it" being Vermouth).

4. After Martini and Rossi Vermouth, because it was first used in the drink, Gin and It, with $\frac{1}{2}$ Gin and $\frac{1}{2}$ Martini and Rossi Vermouth.

5. At the Knickerbocker Hotel in the early 1900s, a Bartender named Martini di Arma Tiggia mixed a Martini using only a dry Gin and only dry Vermouth.

TOP "10"
INTRODUCTION/INSTRUCTIONS

*All recipes have been alphabetized for
your convenience.*

1. Shake, stir, swirl, strain, or whatever. It's really up to you.

2. Some drinks have the same (not many) ingredients, but different names, pick your favorite.

3. If you have trouble finding an ingredient, omit it and go on with your life.

4. If the recipe does not have measurements, use your own taste.

5. Do not flame any drink.

6. Don't drink and drive.

7. Always use "The Best" ingredients.

8. For more information: WWW.BARTENDER.COM

9. Vermouth: French = white/dry; Italian = red/sweet.

10. Have a great life, enjoy your Martini, and thank you for buying the book.

THE MARTINI
FROM
A TO Z

A BALLY GOOD MARTINI

 2 oz. Bombay Sapphire
 1/8 oz. Dry Vermouth
 1/8 oz. Grand Marnier
Garnish with an orange twist.
Bally's
Las Vegas, NV

A BENTLEY MARTINI

 1 oz. Sweet Vermouth
 2 oz. Calvados
Place in shaker with good quantity of
cubed ice. Shake or stir to taste. Strain
into "up" prechilled glass. Garnish with
twist of lemon zest.
Tim Worstall
San Luis Obispo, CA

A PEACHINI MARTINI

 2 cups of fresh skinned peaches
 3 oz. Vodka
sm. scoop Crushed Ice
Blend till smooth.
Jill Stevens
Trabuco Canyon, CA

A.1 MARTINI
    2 oz. Dry Gin
    1 oz. Grand Marnier or Cointreau
    1 tsp. Lemon Juice
    1/2 tsp. Grenadine syrup
Shake and strain.

ABOUT THAT TIME
    2 1/2 oz. Alizé
    1 dash Grenadine
Serve chilled in martini glass.
Garnish with Strawberry.
Iris Vourlatos
E-mail

ABSOLUT HURRICANE WARNING
    1 1/2 oz. Absolut Vodka
    2 oz. Pineapple and Cranberry Juice
Garnish with maraschino cherry.
Hurricane Restaurant
Passagrille, FL

ABSOLUTLY FABULOUS MARTINI

   1¼ oz. Absolut Citron Vodka
   1¼ oz. Absolut Kurant Vodka
      1 Lemon twist for garnish
Stir with ice and strain into a chilled martini glass. Garnish with lemon twist.
The Martini Club
Atlanta, GA

ACE MARTINI

   1½ oz. Dry Gin
    ½ oz. Martini & Rossi Dry
         Vermouth
    ½ oz. Grenadine syrup
   1½ oz. Cream
   1 tsp. Egg White
Shake and strain.

ACID RAIN

   1 part Rain Vodka chilled
   1 part Grapefruit Juice chilled
Strain into martini glass. Garnish with twist of lime.

ACROPOLIS MARTINI

    1¾ oz. Smirnoff Vodka
    ¼ oz. Ouzo 12

Strain and garnish with a black olive.

ADAM & EVE MARTINI

    1 oz. Dry Gin
    1 oz. Forbidden Fruit Liqueur
    1 oz. Cognac
    1 tsp. Lemon Juice

Shake and strain.

ADDISON MARTINI

    1 oz. Dry Gin
    1½ oz. Martini and Rossi Sweet
             Vermouth

Shake and Strain. Decorate with maraschino cherry.

ADIOS AMIGOS MARTINI

    1 oz. Dry Gin
    ½ oz. Brandy
    ½ oz. White Rum
    ½ oz. Martini and Rossi Sweet
             Vermouth
    ½ oz. Lemon Juice

Shake and strain.

ADMIRAL MARTINI

    1 oz. Bourbon
  1½ oz. Dry Vermouth
   ½ oz. Fresh lemon juice
          Lemon twist

Shake liquid ingredients with ice. Strain into chilled cocktail glass. Drop in lemon twist.

ADONIS COCKTAIL

    1 oz. Fino Sherry (Tio Pepe
           or La Ina)
    1 oz. Martini & Rossi Sweet
           Vermouth
    1 oz. Fresh squeezed orange juice
 1 dash Angostura Bitters

Shake all ingredients with ice. Strain into chilled cocktail glass. Garnish with orange peel.

Dale DeGroff
New York, NY

AFFINITY MARTINI

    1 oz. Scotch
    1 oz. Dry Vermouth
    1 oz. Sweet Vermouth
 2 dashes Angostura Bitters

Stir liquid ingredients with ice. Strain into chilled glass. Garnish with maraschino cherry.

AFFINITY MARTINI II

    1 oz. Scotch
    1 oz. Dry Sherry
    1 oz. Ruby Port
 2 dashes Angostura or Orange Bitters
          Maraschino Cherry

AFTER THE FROST MARTINI

        Mission Hill Grand
        Reserve Ice Wine
        Bombay Gin or
        Finlandia Vodka

Garnish with frozen Riesling grapes. Serve in an ice martini glass set over dry ice.

900 West in the Canadian Pacific Hotel Vancouver, B.C.

AFTER-DINNER MARTINI

  2 oz. Stolichnaya Kafya Vodka
  1/4 oz. Stolichnaya Vanil or Stoli
        Zinamon Vodka
Garnish with several coffee beans.

AFTER-GLOW MARTINI

  1 part Melon Liqueur
  2 parts Vodka
  1 part Orange Juice
Served very cold with a dash of lemon.

AGATINI

  2 shots Absolut Citron Vodka
  splash of Chambord
Strain into sugar rimmed martini glass.
Garnish with a twist.
Patty Nolletti
Agatina's Restaurant
Rochester, NY

AGNESE'S GOLDENROD MARTINI

       Tanqueray Gin
       Martini & Rossi Extra Dry
       Vermouth
  drop Grand Marnier

Add a rod of lemon and orange.

Orso's
Chicago, IL

AIR TRAFFIC CONTROL

  1 part Courvoisier VSOP
  1 part White Creme de Menthe
       Lemon twist

The Windsock Bar & Grill
San Diego, CA

ALASKA MARTINI

  2 oz. Dry Gin
  1½ oz. Lemon Juice
  1 tsp. Sugar

Shake and strain into tall glass. Float on top 1 tsp. raspberry syrup or 1 tsp. Creme de Cassis.

ALASKA MARTINI II
    $1\frac{1}{2}$ Dry Gin
    $\frac{1}{2}$ Yellow Chartreuse
Shake and strain.

ALGONQUIN MARTINI
    2 oz. Blended Whiskey
    1 oz. Dry Vermouth
    1 oz. Unsweetened Pineapple Juice
Shake ingredients with ice. Strain into
chilled cocktail glass or serve over ice
cubes in an old-fashioned glass.
Algonquin Hotel
New York, NY

ALIZÉ CARIBBEAN MARTINI
    2 oz. Alizé
    $\frac{1}{2}$ oz. Bacardi Limón
Fill shaker with ice, add above ingredients, cover and shake. Strain ice cold
into martini glass. Garnish with
lemon slice.

ALIZÉ MARTINI

    $1\frac{1}{2}$ oz. Alizé
    $\frac{1}{2}$ oz. Absolut Vodka

Fill shaker with ice, add above ingredients, cover martini shaker and shake. Strain "ice cold" into martini glass. Garnish with thin slice of lemon.

ALIZÉ NECTAR

    $1\frac{1}{2}$ oz. Alizé
    $\frac{1}{2}$ oz. Amaretto
    $\frac{1}{2}$ oz. Rum
    $\frac{1}{2}$ oz. Vodka
    1 oz. Grenadine

Mix ingredients in shaker, shake and strain into tall glass.

ALIZÉ PASSIONATE MARTINI

    2 oz. Alizé
    $\frac{1}{2}$ oz. Absolut Vodka
    $\frac{1}{2}$ oz. Cranberry Juice

Shake and strain.

ALIZÉ RED PASSION MARTINI

2½ oz. Alizé Red Passion
1 oz. Super Premium Vodka

Fill martini shaker ¾ with ice. Add above ingredients. Strain ice cold into martini glass. Garnish with relatively thin slice of lime.

Alizé de France

ALIZÉ TROPICAL MARTINI

2 oz. Alizé
½ oz. Malibu

Fill shaker with ice, add above ingredients, cover and shake. Garnish with maraschino cherry.

ALL TOO IMPORTANT MARTINI

touch Dry Vermouth
2½ oz. Tangueray Gin
2 Olives for garnish

Pour Vermouth into a chilled glass and swirl it around. Dump the Vermouth into the sink. Chill the Tanqueray Gin until cold and strain into the glass. Garnish with the two olives skewered on a pick.

Johnny Love's
San Francisco, CA

ALLIES MARTINI

    1 oz. Gin
    1 oz. Dry Vermouth
 2 dashes Kummel
Stir or shake with ice. Strain into
chilled glass.

ALOHA MARTINI

    2 oz. Smirnoff Vodka
    1/4 oz. Pineapple Juice
    1/4 oz. Apricot Brandy
Chill, strain and garnish with a pineapple wedge.

ALTERNATIVE MARTINI

    2 oz. Absolut Citron Vodka
    1/2 oz. Grand Marnier
Chill and strain into martini glass.
Garnish with lemon twist.
James Allison, Jr.
Boise, ID

ALTERNATINI MARTINI

Rim Martini glass in chocolate fudge.

3 oz.	Tanqueray Sterling Vodka
splash	Martini & Rossi Extra Dry Vermouth
splash	Martini & Rossi Rosso Vermouth
½ oz.	White Creme de Cacao

Garnish with Reese's Peanut Butter Cup.

Jilly's Bistro
Chicago, IL

AMBASSADOR MARTINI

2 oz.	Smirnoff Vodka
dash	Melon Liqueur
dash	Orange Juice

Chill, strain and garnish with an orange wheel.

AMBER DREAM MARTINI

2 parts	Dry Gin
1 part	Italian Vermouth
1 dash	Orange Bitters
3 dashes	Yellow Chartreuse

Shake.

AMBER MARTINI

    1 oz. Vodka
    ½ oz. Amaretto
    ½ oz. Hazelnut Liqueur

Chill, strain and serve in a chilled martini glass.

AMERICAN BEAUTY MARTINI

    1 oz. Brandy
    1 oz. Dry Vermouth
    ¼ oz. Fresh Orange Juice
2 dashes White Creme de Menthe
  1 dash Grenadine
    ½ oz. Ruby Port

Shake all ingredients except Port. Strain into chilled glass. Float Port on top.

AMERICAN PIE MARTINI

    2 oz. Skyy Vodka
    ¼ oz. Stoli Zinamon Vodka
    ¼ oz. Calvados

Garnish with a small wedge of apple. Dip side of the apple slice in cinnamon, Cut a small slice into it so that it fits onto the rim of the glass.

AMERICANO

2 parts Martini & Rossi Sweet
          Vermouth
1 part Campari

Pour over ice and stir. Serve in tall glass
topped with club soda.

AMETHYST
MARTINI

2 oz. Ketel One Vodka
½ oz. Campari
½ oz. Chambord
splash Lime Juice

AMIDES
MARTINI

2 oz. Stolichnaya Vodka
½ oz. Godiva Liqueur
splash Frangelico

Garnish with an almond or hazelnut.

AN IRISH MEXICAN IN RUSSIAN VANILLA FIELDS

    1 oz. Stoli Vanil Vodka
    ½ oz. Baileys Irish Cream
    ½ oz. Kahlua
            Half and Half
  scoop Vanilla Ice Cream
   dash Cinnamon

Mix all ingredients except cinnamon in blender.

Stephanie Meagher-Garcia
Chilli's Bar & Grill
Miami, FL

ANGEL MARTINI

  1½ oz. Ketel One Vodka
   ½ oz. Frangelico

Shake ingredients with ice. Strain into a chilled martini glass.

ANGELINA CLASSY LADY

   2 oz. Bacardi Limón
   ⅛ oz. Rose's Lime Juice
   ½ oz. 7 Up or Sprite
   ⅛ oz. Martini & Rossi Extra
            Dry Vermouth

"WOULD YOU CARE TO JOIN ME
IN A GIN MARTINI?"

ANNAWANNA
TROPICAL MARTINI

  1 oz. Malibu Coconut Rum
  ½ oz. Pineapple Juice
  splash Rose's Lime Juice
  dash Salt

Shake, add ice, shake again, and strain
into chilled martini glass. Garnish
with fruit.

ANTINI MARTINI

  2 oz. Stolichnaya Cristall Vodka
  ½ oz. Lillet Rouge
    1 Burnt Orange twist for
        garnish

Shake with ice and strain into a chilled
martini glass. Garnish with ice burnt
orange twist.

Harry Denton's Starlight Room
San Francisco, CA

APPLE JACK MARTINI

Muddled apple & cinnamon shaken
with Ketel One Vodka. Served with a
sugared cinnamon rim.

Lot 61
New York, NY

APPLE KISS MARTINI
　　¾ oz.　Vodka
　　¾ oz.　Sour Apple Pucker
　½ scoop　Ice
　　splash　Sour Mix
Blend and serve frozen in chilled martini glass. Rim with lime green sugar. Garnish with wedge of apple.
Pamela Conaway
Hurricane Restaurant
Passagrille, FL

APPLE MARTINI
　1½ oz.　Glacier Vodka
　½ part　Schoenauer Apfel Schnapps
　　dash　Cinnamon
Garnish with a slice of apple.

APPLE OF MY EYE
　　1 oz.　Rain Vodka
　　¾ oz.　Apple Brandy
　　¼ oz.　Lime Juice
　　¼ oz.　Grenadine
Chill and serve up in martini glass.

APPLE SAUCE MARTINI

           Chilled Finlandia Vodka
    1/4 oz. Apple Brandy
Finlandia Fashion Martinis

APPLETINI

    1 1/2 oz. Ketel One Vodka
      2 oz. Sour Apple Pucker
Served in chilled martini glass. Garnish
with a round slice of apple.
Bobby McGee's
San Bernardino, CA

APPLETINI II

    3 parts Bombay Gin
    1 part Midori
    splash Pineapple Juice
    splash Sweet & Sour
Shake hard with cut up apple chunks.
Garnish with apple slice.
Mike Simpson
Il Fornaio
San Diego, CA

APRES-SKITINI

    2 oz. Stoli Zinamon Vodka
    splash Mulled Cider

Serve in a warm martini glass with a cinnamon stick.

APRICOT MARTINI

    1 part Godiva Liqueur
    1 part Absolut Vodka
    1 part Apricot Brandy

Combine with ice, shake well. Serve chilled with a maraschino cherry.

APRIL RAIN MARTINI

    1½ oz. Rain Vodka
    3 dashes Triple Sec and Sour Mix
    splash Cranberry Juice

Shake with ice. Strain into martini glass. Garnish with lemon slice.

AQUAMAN MARTINI

    1 oz. Aquavit
    1 oz. Gin
    dash Dry Vermouth

Stir with ice, garnish with olive.

AQUARELLE MARTINI

    2 oz. Bacardi Limón
    1 oz. Ketel One Vodka
    ½ oz. Prunella Sauvage
           (local product)
  Couple of drops of Blue Curacao
           Lemon twist
John Hyde, Bartender
The Watergate Hotel
Washington, DC

AQUAVIT MARTINI

    3 oz. Aquavit – OP.
 few drops Dry Vermouth

ARCADIANA BARTENDER'S FAVORITE MARTINI

    2 oz. Absolut Citron Vodka
           Sweet Vermouth
           Lime Wedge
Shake with Vermouth and lime wedge,
add Vodka, and strain.
Stephanie Guidry
Arcadiana's Catfish Shark
Lafayette, LA

ARISTICRATICO

     Cuervo 1800 Tequila
hint Grand Marnier
     Jalapeño

No. 18
New York, NY

ARLENIE MARTINI

1 oz. Gin
2 oz. Limoncello
1 oz. Frangelico
dash Rum

Shake with ice and strain into 4 oz.
martini glass.
Steve Visakay
Vintage Cocktail Shakers

ARMY COCKTAIL MARTINI

2 oz. Dry Gin
½ oz. Sweet Vermouth
       Orange peel

ARTILLERY MARTINI

2 oz. Gin
1 oz. Sweet Vermouth

Shake ingredients with ice. Strain into
chilled glass.

ASTORIA MARTINI

1½ oz. Dry Gin
¾ oz. Dry Vermouth
1 dash Orange Bitters
Green olive

ATTA BOY MARTINI

2 oz. Dry Gin
½ oz. Dry Vermouth
2 dashes Grenadine

ATTITUD E-TINI

Absolut Citron Vodka
Cointreau
Fresh Lemon Juice
Sugar rimmed glass

The Diner on Sycamore
Cincinnati, OH

ATTY MARTINI

2 oz. Dry Gin
½ oz. Dry Vermouth
2 dashes Creme de Violette
twist Lemon Peel

AUTUMN MARTINI

Stoli Zinamon Vodka

Flavor with Amaretto Liqueur. Garnish
with Orange slice.

Renaissance Atlanta Hotel
Atlanta, GA

AVIATOR MARTINI

Tanqueray Citrus Vodka
splash Cranberry Juice
Lemon Mix
Lemon Wedge

The Windsock Bar & Grill
San Diego, CA

B. R. MARTINI

1½ oz. Stoli Vanil Vodka
½ oz. Kahlua
splash Cream

Garnish with chocolate mint stir.

John Del Giorno
Mirage
Las Vegas, NV

B.V.D. MARTINI
   ¾ oz. Bacardi Light Rum
   ¾ oz. Vermouth (dry)
   ¾ oz. Dubonnet
Stir ingredients with ice. Strain into
chilled glass.

BABE RUTH MARTINI
Fill mixing glass with ice
   ½ oz. Absolut Vodka
   ¾ oz. Dark Creme de Cacao
   ¾ oz. Butterscotch Schnapps
Stir and strain into chilled glass.
Garnish with miniature Baby Ruth.
Chris "Barman" Davis
Lodge at Lakeview
Austin, TX

BACARDI DRY MARTINI
   2 oz. Bacardi Light Rum
   ½ oz. Martini & Rossi Dry
          Vermouth
Shake with ice and strain.

BACARDI LIMÓN MARTINI

  2 oz. Bacardi Limón
  $3/4$ oz. Martini & Rossi Extra Dry
      Vermouth
 splash Cranberry Juice
Shake with ice and strain into
chilled martini glasses. Garnish
with lemon twist.

BACARDI SPICE CARIBBEAN MARTINI

  $2\frac{1}{2}$ oz. Bacardi Spice Rum
  $\frac{1}{2}$ oz. Creme de Banana
Shake and strain over ice. Serve straight
up. Garnish with Pineapple wedge
or cube.

BACARDI SWEET MARTINI

  2 oz. Bacardi Light Rum
      Martini & Rossi Sweet
      Vermouth
Shake with ice and strain.

BAD APPLE MARTINI

  1½ oz. Absolut Citron Vodka
   ½ oz. Berentzen Apfel Liqueur
  2 drops Tabasco Sauce

Chill, shake and strain Absolut into chilled martini glass. Pour Berentzen down side of glass. Pour two drops of Tabasco in center. Garnish with apple slice.
The Country Barrel Inn
Crosswicks, NJ

BAILEY'S CHOCOLATE MARTINI

  1½ parts Baileys Irish Cream
   1 part Stolichnaya Vodka
   ½ part Creme de Cacao

Garnish with a maraschino cherry.

BALD HEAD MARTINI

  4 parts Beefeater Gin
  1 part French Vermouth
  1 part Italian Vermouth
  2 dashes Pernod

Stir gently with ice. Strain or serve on the rocks. Sprinkle the oil from a twist of lemon peel on top.

BALLANTINE'S COCKTAIL

1 1/2 oz. Dry Gin
3/4 oz. French Vermouth
1 dash Orange Bitters
1 dash Pernod

BALLET RUSSE

2 oz. Stolichnaya Vodka
1/4 oz. Chambord
1/4 oz. Sour Mix

The Diner on Sycamore
Cincinnati, OH

BAMBOU'S LIMÓN MARTINI

1/2 oz. Martini & Rossi Extra Dry
Vermouth
2 oz. Bacardi Limón
1 oz. Midori
Lemon twist

Reebok Sports Clubs

BANANA MARTINI

2 1/2 oz. Gordon's Vodka
1/4 oz. Creme de Banana
splash Extra Dry Vermouth
Caramelized banana garnish.

BANANA SPLIT MARTINI

   1 oz. Chilled Finlandia Arctic
            Cranberry Vodka
  1/4 oz. Banana Liqueur
  1/4 oz. Chambord

Finlandia Vodka Americas, Inc.
New York, NY

BANZAI MARTINI

Rinse glass with Martini & Rossi Extra
Dry Vermouth
  2 3/4 oz. Skyy Vodka
    1/4 oz. Sake
Garnish with Japanese pickled plum
and shiso.

Betelnut
San Francisco, CA

BARBARELLA

  2 oz. Vodka
  splash Vermouth
         Gorgonzola stuffed olives

Wolfgang Puck Express
Walt Disney World Resort, FL

BARBED WIRE

　2½ oz. Vodka
　¼ oz. Martini & Rossi Rosso
　　　　 Vermouth
　splash Pernod
　splash Chambord

Garnish with a maraschino cherry.
Harris'
San Francisco, CA

BARNUM MARTINI

　1½ oz. Gin
　½ oz. Apricot Brandy
4 dashes Angostura Bitters
　¼ tsp. Fresh Lemon Juice

Shake ingredients with ice. Strain into
chilled glass.

BARON MARTINI

　1½ oz. Dry Gin
　½ oz. French Vermouth
　¼ oz. Orange Curacao
　¼ oz. Sweet Vermouth

Twist of lemon peel.

BARRY MARTINI

    1½ oz. Dry Gin
    ¾ oz. Sweet Vermouth
    1 dash Angostura Bitters
            White Creme de Menthe

Stir into glass. Float Creme de Menthe on top. Garnish with twist of lemon peel.

BEAN MACHINE

    1 oz. Chilled Finlandia Vodka
    ½ oz. Kahlua

Finlandia Vodka Americas, Inc.
New York, NY

BEAUTY SPOT MARTINI

    1 dash Grenadine
    1 oz. Gin
    ½ oz. Dry Vermouth
    ½ oz. Sweet Vermouth
    1 tsp. Fresh Orange Juice

Put Grenadine in bottom of chilled glass. Shake remaining ingredients with ice. Strain into glass — don't stir.

"THEY'RE OLIVES. BUT WHAT ARE
THEY GOOD FOR?"

BECCO'S MARTINI

   1½ oz. Stoli Ohranj Vodka
   1½ oz. Campari
   ½ oz. Martini & Rossi Sweet
           Vermouth
           Orange peel
Reebok Sports Clubs

BEEFEATER MARTINI

   5 oz. Chilled Beefeater Gin
   1 oz. Dry Vermouth
   4 fat Pimento stuffed Spanish
          olives

The secret to preparation is decisive
quickness, so as not to weaken the spirits with melted ice. Prep your jiggers
and Martini glasses first. Fill a cocktail
pitcher with hard ice cubes, Vermouth,
then Beefeater. Turn the stirrer eight
times only. Strain into glasses. Add olives.

BEE'S KNEES MARTINI

    2 oz. Dry Gin
    1 oz. Lemon Juice
    1 oz. Clear Honey
Shake and strain.

BEL-AIR MARTINI

    ½ oz. Sherry
    2 oz. Vodka
Lemon twist garnish.

BELLINI MARTINI

            Stolichnaya Vodka
            Fresh White Peach Puree
            Zest of lemon
Martini's
New York, NY

BELLINSKY

        3 oz. Pureed Peaches
        1 tsp. Maraschino Cherry Juice or
                to taste
        1 oz. Stoli Persik Vodka
                Brut Champagne

Puree ripe peaches by forcing them
through a sieve. Spoon into a large
chilled wine goblet. Sweeten to taste
with maraschino cherry juice. Add
Vodka and fill with cold Champagne.

BENNETT COCKTAIL MARTINI

    1½ oz. Gin
        2 tsp. Fresh Lime Juice
        1 tsp. Powered Sugar
    2 dashes Angostura or
                Orange Bitters

Shake ingredients with ice. Strain into
chilled glass.

BERI-BERI NICE
    1 part Stoli Strasberi Vodka
    1 part Stoli Razberi Vodka
    splash Chambord
Garnish with fresh raspberry.
Peggy Howell
Cotati Yacht Club & Saloon
Cotati, CA

BERMUDA HIGHBALL MARTINI
    1 oz. Gin
    1 oz. Dry Vermouth
    1 oz. Brandy
           Cold club soda or Ginger ale
           Lemon twist
Put 2 to 3 ice cubes in chilled glass. Add
Gin, Vermouth and Brandy. Top with
club soda or Ginger ale, stirring gently.
Drop in lemon.

BERMUDIANA ROSE
    2 oz. Cork dry Gin
    ¼ oz. Apricot Brandy
    ¼ oz. Grenadine
    ¼ oz. Lemon Juice
Shake.

BERRY BERRY MARTINI
2 oz. Beefeater Gin
½ oz. Cranberry Juice Cocktail
Shake and strain into chilled martini
glass. Garnish with a fresh berry.

BERRY MOCHA MARTINI
1½ oz. Stoli Razberi Vodka
¼ oz. Godiva Chocolate Liqueur
¼ oz. Kahlua
Garnish with raspberries or chocolate.
Keely Kurtas
Allentown Bartender School
Whitehall, PA

BIG APPLE MARTINI
3 oz. Finlandia Vodka
½ oz. Green Apple Schnapps
1½ oz. Sweet & Sour Mix
Garnish with paper thin wafer of
green apple.
Bubble Lounge
San Francisco, CA

BIJOU COCKTAIL MARTINI

    1 oz. Gin
    1 oz. Sweet Vermouth
    1 oz. Green Chartreuse
 1 dash Orange Bitters

Stir liquid ingredients with ice. Strain into chilled glass. Garnish with maraschino cherry.

BIKINI MARTINI

    ⅓ Absolut Citron Vodka
    ⅓ Malibu Rum
    ⅓ Pineapple Juice

Garnish with pineapple flag.
Key Club Hollywood
Hollywood, CA

BITCHIN' MARTINI

   1½ oz. Gin
    ½ oz. Dry Vermouth
1-2 dashes Creme de Menthe
1-2 dashes Pernod
 1 twist Lemon

Stir and serve.

BITTERSWEET MARTINI

  1½ oz. Dry Vermouth
  1½ oz. Sweet Vermouth
  1 dash Angostura Bitters
  1 dash Orange Bitters
          Orange twist

Shake liquid ingredients with ice. Strain into chilled glass. Drop in orange twist.

BLACK CURRANT MARTINI

  1 oz. Godiva Liqueur
  1 oz. Seagram's Gin
  ¼ oz. Creme de Cassis
  ¼ oz. Lemon Juice
  ¼ oz. Lime Juice

Combine ingredients with ice. Shake well, and strain into cocktail glass. Garnish with maraschino cherry.

BLACK EYED "P"

          Absolut Peppar Vodka

Garnish with black olives.
Cecilia's
Breckenridge, CO

BLACK MAGIC

      Jagermeister
      Vodka

Chilled and served straight up.

BLACK MARTINI

1½ oz. Absolut Kurant Vodka
splash Chambord

Stir ingredients and serve straight up or over ice.

BLUE BEEFEATER

3 oz. Beefeater Gin
¼ oz. Vermouth
1 oz. Blueberry Juice (blend
       and strain blueberries
       and lemon)

Coat ice in a shaker with Vermouth and drain excess. Add Beefeater, blueberry juice and a squeeze of lemon. Shake well and strain into martini glass. Sink 3 blueberries and float a twist of lemon for garnish.

BLUE MOON MARTINI

3 oz. Gin or Vodka
2-3 dashes Blue Curacao

BLACK MARTINI

Absolut Kurant Vodka
splash of Chambord
Continental Cafe
Philadelphia, PA

BLACK MARTINI II

Absolut Vodka
Kahlua
shot Chilled Espresso
whisk Cream
Serve in oversized chilled stem.

BLACK STALLION MARTINI

2 oz. Smirnoff Vodka
dash Romana Black Sambuca
Chill, strain and sprinkle with 3 espresso beans.

BLACK TIE MARTINI
    1½ oz. Skyy Vodka
    spritz Campari
    spritz Chivas
        2 Cocktail Onions
        1 Black Olive

BLACKBERRY MARTINI
        Stoli Vanil Vodka
        Chambord
Tunnel Bar Raphael
Providence, RI

BLACKTHORN MARTINI
    1½ oz. Sloe Gin
        1 oz. Sweet Vermouth
    2 dashes Bitters
Stir and strain into chilled glass.
Garnish with lemon twist.

BLAZING IRIS

    2 oz. Vincent Vodka
    1/2 oz. Chambord

Combine ingredients, shake, and strain into a martini glass. Garnish with caramelized lime pinwheels.

Andy Porter
Van Gogh's Restaurant & Bar
Atlanta, GA

BLEU MARTINI

    Fris Vodka
    Dry Vermouth

Garnish with olives stuffed with Bleu Cheese.

BLEEDING HEART MARTINI

Chill bottle of Campari in freezer until it gets syrupy. Wet and chill cocktail glass in freezer as well. Pour 6 oz. Ketel One Vodka into mixing glass with ice. Swirl, and strain into chilled cocktail glass. Slowly pour Campari around rim of glass. Garnish with black olive.

Thomas Rozycki
Bloomsburg, PA

BLENTON MARTINI

    1½ oz. Dry Gin
    ¾ oz. Dry Vermouth
    1 dash Angostura Bitters
Twist of lemon peel.

BLIMLET MARTINI

    2 oz. Dry Gin
    2 oz. Rose's Lime Juice
    1 oz. Lemon Juice
    ½ oz. Creme de Cassis

BLONDE MARTINI

Bombay Sapphire
Enlivened with Lillet Blonde.
Brasserie Jo Martini's
Chicago, IL

BLOOD AND SAND MARTINI

    ¾ oz. Scotch
    ¾ oz. Cherry Brandy
    ¾ oz. Sweet Vermouth
    ¾ oz. Fresh Orange Juice
Shake ingredients with ice. Strain into
chilled glass.

BLOOD OHRANJ MARTINI

 3 parts Stoli Ohranj Vodka
 1 part Campari
 splash Club Soda

Stir ingredients with ice.

BLOODHOUND MARTINI

 1 oz. Gin
 ½ oz. Dry Vermouth
 ½ oz. Sweet Vermouth
 ½ oz. Strawberry Liqueur

Shake liquid ingredients with ice.
Strain into chilled glass. Garnish with
strawberry.

BLOODY MARTINI

 2 oz. Smirnoff Vodka
 dash Tomato Juice

Generous shake of Worcestershire Sauce
and Tabasco. Chill and strain into a
martini glass. Top with freshly grated
horseradish and garnish with a lime.

BLUE DOLPHIN MARTINI

    2 oz. Chilled Finlandia Vodka
    ¼ oz. Blue Curacao
    ¼ oz. Grand Marnier
    1 oz. Grapefruit Juice
 2 drops Rose's Lime Juice

BLUE EYED TOMCAT

Bombay Sapphire Gin martini dressed
with tomolives.
Cecilia's
Breckenridge, CO

BLUE GORDON'S MARTINI

         Gordon's Vodka
         Blue Curacao
  twist Lemon

BLUE WATER

    2 oz. Skyy Vodka
    ¼ oz. Blue Curacao
Shake. Serve up or on the rocks.
Saba Blue Water Café
Austin, TX

BLUE LAGOON MARTINI

   1¼ oz. Bacardi Limón
   ½ oz. Blue Curacao
   ¼ oz. Dry Vermouth

Garnish with strawberry or olives.

Alex Refojo
Club Mystique
Miami, FL

BLUE MARTINI

   1 oz. Stoli Limonnaya Vodka
   1 oz. Stoli Razberi Vodka
  splash Sour Mix
   dash Curacao

Garnish with lemon twist.

BLUE MONDAY MARTINI

   1½ oz. Smirnoff Vodka
   ¾ oz. Triple Sec
   dash Blue Curacao

Chill, strain and garnish with an
orange slice.

"TWO OLIVES! WHO DO YOU KNOW?"

BLUE PERIOD MARTINI

Absolut Vodka
Leyden Gin
Blue Curacao

Pineapple juice and a splash of Sprite.

Martini Club
Atlanta, GA

BLUE ROOM MARTINI

4 oz. Stoli Persik Vodka
splash Sour Mix
splash Blue Curacao

Shake and add twist.

BLUE SAPPHIRE MARTINI

splash Dry Vermouth
3 oz. Bombay Sapphire Gin
1 oz. Blue Curacao

Stir with ice and strain into a
chilled martini glass. Garnish with a
maraschino cherry.

The Mandarin
San Francisco, CA

BLUE SHARK MARTINI

   1 1/2 oz. Vodka
   1 1/2 oz. Tequila
   1/2 oz. Blue Curacao
Shake ingredients with ice. Strain into
chilled martini glass or over ice.

BLUE SKYY MARTINI

   2 1/2 oz. Skyy Vodka
   splash Blue Curacao
Stir with ice and strain into chilled
martini glass.
Compass Rose
San Francisco, CA

BLUES MARTINI

   1/2 oz. Ketel One Vodka
   1/2 oz. Bombay Sapphire Gin
few drops Blue Curacao
Stir gently with ice. Serve straight up or
over ice.

BOBBY BURNS MARTINI

1½ oz. Scotch
1½ oz. Sweet Vermouth
1½ tsp. Benedictine

Stir and strain into chilled glass.
Garnish with lemon twist.

BOMBAY MARTINI

3 oz. Bombay Gin
splash Martini & Rossi Dry
            Vermouth

Garnish with Blue Cheese Olive.
Gibson's
Chicago, IL

BONNIE PRINCE MARTINI

1½ oz. Dry Gin
½ oz. Lillet
¼ oz. Drambuie

BOOKMARK

Ketel One Vodka
dash Chambord

Garnish with a Tomolive.

BOOMERANG MARTINI

  4 parts Dry Gin
   1 part French Vermouth
   1 part Italian Vermouth
 2 dashes Maraschino Cherry Juice
Twist of lemon peel.

BORU MARTINI

Fill shaker with ice. Add desired
amount of Boru Original Vodka. Add
splash of Boru Orange or Citrus Vodka.
Shake gently and strain into chilled
Martini glass. Garnish with orange or
lemon peel.

BOSTON BULLET MARTINI

  2 oz. Dry Gin
  ½ oz. Dry Vermouth
Garnish with Almond-stuffed
green olive.

BOTICELLI MARTINI

  1¼ oz. Bombay Sapphire Gin
  1¼ oz. Ketel One Vodka
Garnish with goat cheese stuffed olive.
Kevin Jason
Restorante Primavera
Millis, MA

BOTTLEGGER MARTINI

> Bombay Gin
> Southern Comfort
> Lemon twist

Chianti
Houston, TX

BOWERY

Equal parts of Godiva Liqueur,
Campari, Ketel One Vodka. Stir and
Serve.

BOXER MARTINI

> 2 oz. Absolut Vodka
> 1 oz. Absolut Peppar Vodka
> ½ oz. Dubonnet Blanc
>   (or Vermouth)

BRANDIED MADEIRA MARTINI

> 1 oz. Brandy
> 1 oz. Madeira
> ½ oz. Dry Vermouth

Stir with ice. Strain into chilled glass
over ice cubes. Garnish with lemon
twist.

BRAVE COW MARTINI

1½ oz. Gin
½ oz. Coffee Liqueur

Chill and strain into a chilled martini glass.

BRAZIL COCKTAIL MARTINI

1½ oz. Dry Vermouth
1½ oz. Dry Sherry
1 dash Angostura Bitters
1 dash Pernod or other Anise-
          Flavored Liqueur

Stir and strain into chilled glass.
Garnish with lemon twist.

BREAKFAST MARTINI

Orange marmalade shaken with Stoli
Ohranj Vodka and zest.
Lot 61
New York, NY

BRONX MARTINI

> Beefeater Gin
> Martini & Rossi Extra Dry
> Vermouth
> Martini & Rossi Rosso
> Vermouth
> Orange Juice

Garnish with twist of lemon.
Mr. Babbington's
New York, NY

BRIT MARTINI

> Beefeater Gin

Blended with Pimm's #1. Garnish with
Cucumber slice.
Polo Lounge
Windsor Court Hotel
New Orleans, LA

BRONX GOLDEN

> Beefeater Gin
> Dry Vermouth
> Sweet Vermouth
> Orange Juice
> Egg Yolk

BRONX TERRACE

   1½ oz. Gin
   ¾ oz. Fresh Lime Juice
   ½ oz. Dry Vermouth
          Maraschino Cherry

Shake with ice. Strain into chilled glass.
Garnish with maraschino cherry.

BROWN COCKTAIL MARTINI

   1 oz. Light Rum
   1 oz. Gin
   ¾ oz. Dry Vermouth

Stir ingredients with ice. Strain into
chilled glass.

BUCKEYE MARTINI

   2 oz. Smirnoff Vodka
   ½ oz. Dry Vermouth

Strain into glass. Garnish with black
olive.

BUFF MARTINI

    5 parts Finlandia Vodka
    1 part Baileys Irish Cream
    1 part Kahlua

Stir gently with ice and strain. Add a sprinkle of freshly ground coffee or cinnamon.

BULLDOG

    1½ oz. Beefeater Gin
    1½ oz. Orange Juice

Stir juice and Gin over ice in collins glass. Fill with Ginger ale. Garnish with maraschino cherry or orange.

BUNNY HUG MARTINI

    1 oz. Dry Gin
    1 oz. Pernod
    1 oz. Whiskey

Shake and strain.

BURNT MARTINI

    1½ oz. Beefeater Gin
    splash Scotch

Shake with ice, strain, and serve with lemon twist.

Anita Sholdice
Qualicum Beach, B.C.

CABARET COCKTAIL

    2 oz. Dry Gin
    ¼ oz. Dry Vermouth
    ¼ oz. Benedictine
  2 dashes Angostura Bitters
Garnish with maraschino cherry.

CABINIERI

    1 oz. Galliano
    1 oz. Cointreau (or triple sec)
    1 Egg Yolk

Pour liqueurs first into mixing glass. Crack egg and separate yolk from egg white. Add yolk to mixing glass. Add OJ. Fill with ice and shake vigorously until all ingredients are fully integrated and mixture is well chilled. Strain into cocktail glass. Garnish with orange wheel.

Frederick C. Thomas
Long Island City, NY

CAJUN KING MARTINI
1-2 dashes Dry Vermouth
    1/2 oz. Absolut Citron Vodka
    1 1/2 oz. Absolut Peppar Vodka
Garnish with a small jalapeño pepper.

CAJUN MARTINI
    2 oz. Stoli Pertsovka Vodka
    1/2 oz. Dry Vermouth
Garnish with a jalapeño pepper.

CAJUN MARTINI II
    Absolut Peppar Vodka
    Dry Vermouth
Garnish with Tomolives.

CAJUN MARTINI III
Put 1 seedless Hot Chili Pepper in a
bottle of Vodka. Let sit for 24 hours.
Soak olives in Tabasco for 10 minutes.
Add 1 1/2 oz. Hot Chili Pepper Vodka.
Dust rim with salt and pepper. Garnish
with hot olives.
Martini Message Board
Ft. Wayne, IN

CALYPSO SPLASH

Leyden Dry Gin
Blue Curacao
splash Pineapple Juice

Red Lobster
Memphis, TN

CAMPARI VICEROY

2 oz. Campari
½ oz. DiSaronno Amaretto
½ oz. Southern Comfort
Pineapple Juice
Orange Juice

Shake well and serve over ice in a highball glass.

CAMPARI MARGIE

3 parts Campari
1 part Triple Sec
1 part Sour Mix
dash Rose's Lime Juice

Shaken and served straight up in a chilled martini glass.

CAMPARI RENAISSANCE

½ parts Campari
½ parts Vodka
½ part Apricot Brandy
        Juice of ½ Orange
        Juice of ½ Tangerine
        Juice of 1 Lemon

Garnish with tangerine slice and lemon twist.

CAMPARTINI

2 oz. Campari
2 oz. Stoli Ohranj Vodka
dash Rose's Lime Juice
splash Orange Juice

Shaken not stirred, served in a chilled martini glass with an orange slice.

CAMPTON COSMO MARTINI

1½ oz. Absolut Citron Vodka
¼ oz. Tuaca
splash Cranberry Juice
½ oz. Lemon Juice
1 Kumquat

Stir with ice and strain into a chilled martini glass. Garnish with the kumquat.

CAMPTON CURE MARTINI

    1 oz. Absolut Citron Vodka
    ½ oz. Cointreau
3 squeezes Lime Juice
    splash Cranberry Juice

Stir with ice and strain into a chilled martini glass.

Campton Place Hotel
San Francisco, CA

CANDY-CANE MARTINI

    Vodka
    Green Creme de Menthe

Serve in a sugar-rimmed glass.

CANTINI

    Skyy Vodka
    Canton Ginger Liqueur

Garnish with candied Ginger. Serve up in an oversized chilled stem. Shaken, not stirred.

CANTON MARTINI

2 oz. Grey Goose Vodka
1/2 oz. Grand Marnier
1/2 oz. Canton Ginger Liqueur

Shake Vigorously. Garnish with a
candied Ginger slice.

Brad Nelson
56 West
Chicago, IL

CAPITOL "G" MARTINI

Gordon's Vodka
Vermouth with Tomolive

CAPOUTINI

2 oz. Leyden Dry Gin
splash Raspberry Puree

Garnish with 3 or 4 raspberries.

Jacques Capsouto
Capsouto Restaurant
New York, NY

CAPRICE MARTINI

1 1/2 oz. Dry Gin
1/2 oz. Dry Vermouth
1/2 oz. Benedictine
1 dash Orange Bitters

CARDAMOM MARTINI

Muddle 8/9 Cardamon seeds with a
large dash of sugar syrup. Add a large
pour of Belvedere Vodka. Shake well.
Strain through a sieve into a martini
glass. Garnish with 3 Cardamom seeds,
if you can find them.
Ben Pundole, General Manager
Lot 61
New York, NY

CARIBE MARTINI

    1 oz. Mt. Gay Rum
    1 oz. Bacardi
Add touch of pineapple.
No. 18
New York, NY

CARNIVAL MARTINI

        Vodka
        Fresh Lime
        Orange Juice
Coconut Grove
San Francisco, CA

CARROLL COCKTAIL MARTINI

1½ oz. Brandy
¾ oz. Sweet Vermouth

Stir liquid ingredients with ice. Strain into chilled glass. Garnish with maraschino cherry.

CARY GRANT

Rinse glass with Martini & Rossi Extra Dry Vermouth. Add 2½ oz. Luksusowa Potato Vodka (Polish Vodka). Splash of Tio Pepe (Dry Sherry). Add ½ oz. fresh lime juice.

Balboa
San Francisco, CA

CASINO COCKTAIL

2 oz. Gin
2 dashes Angostura Bitters
¼ oz. Maraschino Cherry Juice
¼ oz. Lemon Juice

CATALINA MARTINI

2½ oz. Gordon's Vodka
½ oz. Peach Schnapps
½ oz. Extra Dry Vermouth

Garnish with lemon twist soaked in Grand Marnier.

CATHERINE THE GREAT MARTINI

Mixture of Absolut, Cointreau and a dash of Framboise well shaken and topped with Champagne.

CECILIA'S BOLD

Absolut Peppar Vodka
Beefeater Gin
Italian Dry Vermouth

Garnish with Chicago style pepper.
Cecilia's
Breckenridge, CO

CELEBRITY MARTINI

2½ oz. Gin
1 oz. Alizé
½ oz. Grand Marnier

Rinse martini glass with Rose's Lime Juice. Shake remaining ingredients and strain into glass. Garnish with lemon and lime twist.
Chris Golz
Forbidden Fruit
Long Beach, CA

CELTIC MARTINI

Equal parts of Celtic Crossing and Lemon Vodka. Garnish with a lemon twist.

CELTIC CONTINENTAL

	Celtic Crossing
dash	Chambord
splash	Peach Schnapps

Shaken and served chilled in a martini glass.

CENTER OF THE UNIVERSE MARTINI

	Vodka
	Coke
splash	Coffee
splash	Kiwi-strawberry
splash	Tonic
splash	Chocolate Milk

Sasha Nicholas
Princeton, NJ

CHAMPAGNE MARTINI

   1 oz. Finlandia Vodka
  ¼ oz. Chambord
           Peachtree Schnapps
           Korbel Brut Champagne

Chill a Martini glass. Fill a spray bottle with Peachtree Schnapps. In martini shaker, add ice, Finlandia and Chambord. Liberally fill inner surface of Martini glass with Schnapps. Add contents of cocktail shaker and fill remainder of glass with cold champagne. Float one petal from a red rose on the surface and serve.

Rio Suite Hotel and Casino
Las Vegas, NV
F&B VP Craig Gilbert
Sommelier Barrie Levin
Beverage Manager
Dan Collins

CHAMPAGNE ROYALE
DE MARTINI

 1½ oz. Premium Vodka
  1 oz. Veuve Clicquot Yellow Label
     Champagne
 ½ oz. Chambord Raspberry
     Liqueur

Stir with ice and strain into a chilled
martini glass. Garnish with lemon twist.
Tongue & Groove
Atlanta, GA

CHARTRINI
MARTINI

Vodka with a dash of Chartreuse.

CHATTERLY
MARTINI

  2 oz. Dry Gin
 ½ oz. Dry Vermouth
 ¼ oz. Orange Curacao

CHEAP THRILL

        DeKuyper Thrilla Vanilla
        Liqueur
splash Vodka

Served very cold with the glass lightly drizzled with chocolate syrup. Drink is topped with a touch of whipped cream and cinnamon.

CHEKHOV COFFEE MARTINI

Stoli Kafya Vodka with Romana Black Sambuca served straight up.

CHELSEA SIDECAR

2 oz. Beefeater Gin
1/8 oz. Triple Sec
1/8 oz. Lime Juice

CHERRY KISS

1 oz. Vincent Vodka
1/2 oz. Maraschino Cherry Juice
2 oz. Pineapple Juice
2 dashes Grenadine

Combine ingredients, shake, and strain into a martini glass. Top with a bit of grated nutmeg.

Dale DeGroff
New York, NY

CHERRY RIPE MARTINI

Combine 1½ oz. Smirnoff Vodka with ½ oz. Cherry Brandy and ½ oz. Brandy. Strain and garnish with maraschino cherry.

CHERRY TREE

Fresh Maraschino cherries shaken with Skyy Vodka and Cherry Liqueur.

CHESAPEAKE MARTINI

2 oz.	Stoli Pertsovka Vodka
1 tbsp.	Clam or Oyster Liquid
2 dashes	Hot Sauce
½ tsp.	Old Bay Seasoning
1	Cherry Tomato
1	Fresh Oyster

Harbor Court
Baltimore, MD

CHESTERFIELD

       Belvedere Vodka
       Cointreau
       Juice of $\frac{1}{2}$ Fresh Orange
       Juice of $\frac{1}{4}$ Fresh Lemon
  dash Martini & Rossi Extra
       Dry Vermouth
       Sour Mix
  pinch Sugar

Place 1-2 drops of Martini & Rossi
Extra Dry Vermouth in iced cup. Fill
with ice. Add Vodka. Add splash
Cointreau and pinch of sugar. Squeeze
orange juice in and drop the orange
(including rind) into mix. Add splash of
sour mix. Shake until cold. Strain into
chilled glass. Garnish with twist. For
sweet occasions, sugar the rim of the
Martini glass.

Lola's
Chicago, IL

CHICAGO LAKE BREEZE MARTINI

    1½ oz. Stoli Persik Vodka
    splash 7-Up
    splash Cranberry Juice
Garnish with a lemon twist.

CHICAGO MARTINI

    2 oz. Dry Gin
    ½ oz. Scotch
Garnish with green olive.

CHILI PEPPER MARTINI

    scoop Ice
    1¼ oz. Skyy Vodka
    ¼ oz. Goldschlager
Shake well, strain into cold martini glass.

CHILLY WILLY

Chill a martini glass. Fill shaker to top with ice. Add one shot Rumple Minze. One shot Stolichnaya Vodka. Shake and strain.

CHINA BLUE MARTINI

> Gin
> Canton Ginger Liqueur
> Blue Curacao

Finished with large hunk of
crystallized Ginger.
The Martini Club
Atlanta, GA

CHINESE SKYY LINE MARTINI

Skyy Vodka with a chilled sake floater.
Serve up in an oversized chilled stem.
Shaken, not stirred.
Skyy Martini List

CHINOOK MARTINI

Infuse Smirnoff Vodka with 2 parts
fresh raspberries and 1 part fresh blueberries. 2 oz. Infused Smirnoff Vodka,
dash of lime cordial. Chill, strain and
top with fresh berries.

CHOCATINI

> 1¼ oz. Grey Goose Vodka
> ½ oz. White Creme de Cacao

Sid Maples
Julie's Supper Club
San Francisco, CA

CHOCOLATE
CHOO CHOO MARTINI

      Absolut Vodka
      Godiva Chocolate Liqueur
      Kahlua

Garnish with a Chocolate Kiss.

CHOCOLATE COVERED
CHERRY MARTINI

  1$\frac{3}{4}$ oz. Vodka
  $\frac{1}{4}$ oz. White Creme de Cacao
  splash Grand Marnier

Shake and strain into chilled martini
glass. Garnish with a maraschino cherry.

CHOCOLATE COVERED
RASPBERRY

  2 oz. Stoli Razberi Vodka
  1 oz. Godet White Chocolate
        Liqueur

CHOCOLATE GHOST MARTINI

In glass shaker filled ½ with ice add
1 oz. Stoli Vodka, ½ oz. White Creme
de Cacao. Stir & strain into chilled
martini glass, then chill ½ oz. Godet
White Chocolate Liqueur. Strain and
float the Godet.

Toby Ellis
T.G.I. Friday's
Chevy Chase, MD

CHOCOLATE HAZELNUT

> Skyy Vodka shaken with
> Creme de Cacao & Frangelico

Lot 61
New York, NY

CHOCOLATE MARTINI

1 oz. Absolut Vodka
¼ oz. Godiva Chocolate Liqueur
Shake over ice; strain into a chilled glass
with a lemon twist garnish.

CHOCOLATE MARTINI II

 1½ oz. Absolut Kurant Vodka
 dash White Creme de Cacao
Pour Kurant and Creme de Cacao over ice. Shake or stir well. Strain and serve in a chocolate-rimmed cocktail glass straight up or over ice. Garnish with an orange peel.

CHOCOLATE PEPPERMINT MARTINI

 2 oz. Grey Goose Vodka
 1 oz. Chocolate Liqueur
 splash Peppermint Schnapps
Stir and garnish with peppermint stick.

CHOCOLATE RASPBERRY MARTINI

   Belvedere Vodka
   White Chocolate Liqueur
   Dark Chocolate Liqueur
   Martini & Rossi Rosso
   Vermouth
   Raspberry Liqueur
Garnish with fresh raspberry marinated in Vodka.

CHOCOLATINI

   1½ oz. Godiva Dark Chocolate
             Liqueur
   1 oz. Stoli Vanil Vodka

Shake and strain into a chilled martini glass. Garnish with Hershey Kiss or Chocolate dipped cherries or a marshmallow.

CHOCO-RASPBERRY MARTINI

   3 oz. Stoli Vanil Vodka
   3 oz. Stoli Razberi Vodka
   1 oz. Creme de Cacao

Shake and strain into chilled martini glass.

CHOCOTINI

   2 oz. Stoli Ohranj Vodka
   ¼ oz. Godiva Chocolate Liqueur

Serve up or on the rocks. Garnish with orange slice.

Jill Stevens
Trabuco Canyon, CA

CHOCOTINI II

   2 oz. Iced Vodka
   1/2 oz. Chilled Espresso
   splash Dark Creme de Cacao
Garnish with 3 espresso beans and
rimmed with chocolate shavings.

CHOPIN'S #8

   1 1/2 oz. Chopin Vodka
   1/4 oz. Chambord
Shake vigorously. Strain & pour into
frozen cocktail glass. Float 1/4 oz. cranberry juice. Garnish with fresh raspberry (let it sink to the bottom).
Julie Grant
Puzzles
Atlanta, GA

CINNAMON AND SPICE

   2 oz. Bacardi Spice Rum
   1/8 oz. Martini & Rossi Rosso
            Vermouth
Garnish with two cinnamon sticks.
Shaken not stirred.
Red Head's
Chicago, IL

CINNAMON MARTINI

    2 oz. Vodka
    ½ tsp. Goldschlager

Mix Vodka and Goldschlager with
cracked ice. Shake and strain into
chilled martini glass. Garnish with
cinnamon stick and 3 "Red Hots."

Todd Greeno
E-mail

CINNAMON MARTINI II

    3½ oz. Smirnoff Vodka
    dash Cinnamon Schnapps

Chill, strain and garnish with a
cinnamon stick.

CINNAMON TOAST MARTINI

    2 oz. Absolut Vodka
    ¼ oz. Cinnamon Schnapps
    1 Cinnamon Wafer

Line the glass with Cinnamon Schnapps
and pour out excess. Pour the frozen
Absolut Vodka. Stir with wafer and serve.

Jeremy Goring
The Observatory Hotel
Sydney, Australia

CINNAMON TOAST II

1¼ oz. Stoli Zinamon Vodka
¼ oz. Buttershots Schnapps

Top with 1 spoonful or packet of sugar.
Sprinkle with cinnamon.

Andrew Holmes
Jardines
Kansas City, MO

CITRON MARTINI

1¼ oz. Absolut Citron Vodka
dash Extra Dry Vermouth

Pour Citron and Vermouth over ice.
Shake or stir well. Strain and serve in a
cocktail glass, straight up or over ice.
Garnish with a twist or an olive.

CITRON MARTINI II

Absolut Citron Vodka
Chambord

Portland's Best
Portland, OR

CITRON MY FACE

   1 1/2 oz. Absolut Citron Vodka
   splash Rose's Lime Juice
   3/4 oz. Cranberry Juice
   3/4 oz. Pineapple Juice
Shake vigorously, so crystals appear.
Strain and serve.
Greg Chandler
E-mail

CITRONINI

Absolut Citron Vodka complemented
with lemon juice and sour mix. Serve in
sugar rimmed martini glass.
Hurricane Restaurant
Passagrille, FL

CITRUS MARTINI

   3 oz. Stoli Limonnaya Vodka
   3/4 oz. Cointreau
   1/4 oz. Lemon Juice
Pravda
New York, NY

CITRUS-TINI

    2 oz. Absolut Citron Vodka
    1/4 oz. Grand Marnier
    dash Rose's Lime Juice

Garnish with twist of lime/lemon.
Brian Misenheimer
Houlihan's
Greensboro, NC

CLARIDGE MARTINI

    1 oz. Gin
    1 oz. Dry Vermouth
    1/2 oz. Apricot Brandy
    1/2 oz. Triple Sec or Cointreau

Shake with ice. Strain into chilled glass.

CLASSIC DRY

    2 1/2 oz. Bombay Gin
    splash Vermouth
    1 Lemon Twist

The Martini Club
Atlanta, GA

CLASSIC FINTINI

    Chilled Finlandia Vodka

Garnish optional.
Finlandia Fashion Martinis

CLASSIC OLIVE MARTINI
Ketel One Vodka
1 drop each Dry Vermouth and
Olive Juice
Chill until bone-rattling cold. Strain
into glass. Garnish with 3 super-colossal
Sicilian olives.
Jeff Nace
Olives
Boston, MA

CLASSIC VODKA
Chilled Stolichnaya Vodka and
lemon twist garnish.
Renaissance Atlanta Hotel
Atlanta, GA

CLEANHEAD
$1\frac{1}{2}$ oz. Stolichnaya Vodka over ice
Top with tonic and two lime segments.
Squeeze limes well.

CLEMENTINI
Fresh Clementine
Shaken with Stoli Ohranj Vodka and
Grand Marnier.
Lot 61
New York, NY

CLOUDY DAY MARTINI

                Absolut Vodka
    splash Opal Nera
Garnish with espresso bean.

CLOUDY SKIES MARTINI

                Skyy Vodka
    splash Sambuca
                Lemon twist
The Windsock Bar & Grill
San Diego, CA

CLOVE MARTINI

Freshly ground cloves shaken with
Belvedere Vodka.
Lot 61
New York, NY

CLUB COCKTAIL MARTINI

    $1\frac{1}{2}$ oz. Dry Gin
    $\frac{3}{4}$ oz. Sweet Vermouth
    $\frac{1}{4}$ oz. Yellow Chartreuse
Garnish with a maraschino cherry or
green olive.

CLUB LADY'S FAMOUS IN & OUT MARTINI

"Always chill before you fill." Chill 4 to 6 ounces Martini glass. Put in a dash of Martini & Rossi Extra Dry Vermouth and then throw out, thus the name "In and Out." Add Belvedere Vodka to a Martini glass filled with ice. Shake forcefully for about 30 seconds. Strain into Martini glass. Garnish with 2 to 3 Club Lady's exclusive Bleu Cheese Stuffed Spanish Olives and a lemon twist.

Club Lady's
Chicago, IL

CLUB MACANUDO

 2 oz. Grey Goose Vodka
 1/2 oz. Lillet (French Wine)
 splash Grand Marnier

Shake, strain, top off with 1/2 oz. Champagne.

Fernanco Aluardo
Club Macanudo
Chicago, IL

COBALT BLUE MARTINI

   2 oz. Gin
   $1/8$ oz. Blue Curacao
Garnish with lemon twist.

COCOA-BANANA MARTINI

   1 oz. Vodka
   $1/2$ oz. Dark Creme de Cacao
   $1/2$ oz. Banana Liqueur
Rim the martini glass with cocoa powder.

CODE RED MARTINI

   Skyy Vodka
   Grand Marnier
splash Cranberry Juice
Lemon twist garnish.

COFFEE MARTINI

   2 oz. Stoli Kafya Vodka
   $1/8$ oz. DiSaronno Amaretto
splash Sweet Vermouth

COINTINI

2 oz. Stoli Ohranj Vodka
1/8 oz. Cointreau
Brasserie Jo Martini's
Chicago, IL

COINTREAU MARTINI

2 oz. Finlandia Vodka
1/8 oz. Cointreau
Portland's Best
Portland, OR

COLD DECK MARTINI

1 1/2 oz. Brandy
3/4 oz. Sweet Vermouth
1 1/2 tsp. Creme de Menthe
Shake ingredients with ice. Strain into
chilled glass.

COMFORTABLE POSSESSION

1/2 oz. Absolut Citron Vodka
1/2 oz. Southern Comfort
        Lemon twist
Shaken, not stirred.

CONTEMPORARY MARTINI

2 oz. Absolut Citron Vodka
4 drops Cointreau

Fill shaker with ice. Add Vodka and Cointreau. Shake until well chilled and strain into martini glass. Garnish with orange peel.

Top of the Hub
Boston, MA

CONTINENTAL MARTINI

Stolichnaya Vodka
A ghost of Dry Vermouth

Garnish with a lemon stuffed olive.

The Continental Café
Philadelphia, PA

COOPERSTOWN MARTINI

1 oz. Dry Gin
¼ oz. French Vermouth
¼ oz. Italian Vermouth
dash Orange Bitters
dash Angostura

Stir with a sprig of mint and garnish with a twist of lemon.

COPENHAGEN MARTINI

    1 oz. Dry Gin
    1 oz. Aquavit
    1/2 oz. Dry Vermouth
Garnish with a green olive.

COPPER ILLUSION MARTINI

    1/4 oz. Cointreau
    1/4 oz. Campari
    2 1/2 oz. Beefeater Gin
Martini mixing glass filled with ice.
One orange twist for garnish.
Michael Vezzoni
The Four Seasons Olympic Hotel
Seattle, WA

CORAL MARTINI

Combine 2 oz. Smirnoff Citrus Twist
Vodka with 1/3 oz. freshly squeezed
orange juice. Strain into martini glass.
Top with chilled champagne. Garnish
with orange wheel.

CORIANDER MARTINI
Freshly muddled coriander shaken with
pepper and Skyy Vodka.

CORKSCREW MARTINI
   1½ oz. Light Rum
   ½ oz. Dry Vermouth
   ½ oz. Peach Liqueur or Brandy
            Lime Slice
Shake liquid ingredients with ice. Strain
into chilled glass. Garnish with lime.

CORNET MARTINI
   1½ oz. Bombay Gin
   dash Port Wine
Stir in cocktail glass. Strain & serve
straight up or on the rocks. Add lemon
twist or olives.

COSMO KAZI
   1 oz. Stoli Limonnaya Vodka
   ½ oz. Triple Sec
   ½ oz. Lime Juice
   1 oz. Cranberry Juice
   ½ oz. Sweet and Sour Mix
Shake and strain.
Alan Hara
Club Miwa's

COSMO LIMÓN MARTINI

    2 oz. Bacardi Limón
    ½ oz. Cointreau
    ¼ oz. Rose's Lime Juice
    ¾ oz. Cranberry Juice

Shake and strain into chilled martini glass. Garnish with lemon twist.

Safari Lounge
Fort Lee, NJ

COSMOPOLITAN

    1½ oz. OP.
    ½ oz. Triple Sec/Cointreau/
           Grand Marnier
    1 oz. Cranberry Juice

Shake with ice. Serve on the rocks or in a frosted martini glass.

COSMOPOLITAN WAY BACK WHEN!

        Cointreau
        Cranberry and Lime Juice

Garnished with an olive and orange twist.

COSMOPOLITAN MARTINI

    2 oz. Vodka
    1 oz. Cointreau
squeeze ½ lime
  splash Cranberry Juice

Shake with ice. Strain into chilled
martini glass. Garnish with a twist.

COSMOPOLITAN MARTINI II

    ½ oz. Absolut Citron Vodka
    ½ oz. Cointreau
  splash Cranberry Juice
  splash Sprite

Strain over ice into martini stem glass.
Garnish with barbed wire stirrer and
lemon twist.
Brett Andress
Charlotte, NC

COSMOPOLITAN MARTINI III

        Vodka
        Blue Curacao
        Cranberry Juice

Garnish with a lemon twist.
Sheraton Seattle
Seattle, WA

"THIS IS HEAVEN, OF COURSE
THERE'S MARTINIS!"

COSMOPOLITAN IV

    2 oz. Bombay Sapphire Gin
           or Stoli Gold Vodka
    1 oz. Cranberry Juice
  ½ oz. Orange Liqueur
1 splash Fresh Lime Juice
Garnish with lemon twist.

COSMOPOLITINI

           Absolut Citron Vodka
           Cranberry Juice
           Cointreau
           Rose's Lime Juice
Polo Lounge
Windsor Court Hotel
New Orleans, LA

COWBOY MARTINI

           Fresh Mint Leaves
Shaken with sugar and Belvedere
Vodka.
Lot 61
New York, NY

COYOTE MARTINI

    1 liter Tequila

        3 Serrano Chilies

Add chilies to Tequila in the bottle; let sit for 48 hours or more at room temperature. Put Tequila in freezer until thoroughly chilled. Served straight from the freezer in chilled glasses.

The Coyote Café
Santa Fe, NM

CRANBERRY MARTINI

    1 part Godiva Liqueur

    1 part Absolut Vodka

    1 part Cranberry Juice

Combine with ice and shake well. Garnish with a lime twist.

CRANBERRY SAUCE MARTINI

    1 oz. Gordon's Orange Vodka

    ¼ oz. Cranberry Juice

Garnish with cranberries that have been soaked in simple syrup.

CRANTINI

        Finlandia Cranberry Vodka
        Grand Marnier

Portland's Best
Portland, OR

CRANTINI II

    2 oz. Bacardi Limón
  touch Martini & Rossi Extra Dry
        Vermouth
 splash Cranberry Juice

Shake and serve straight up. Garnish
with cranberries and a lemon twist.

CRANTINI III

  1½ oz. Smirnoff Vodka
  1½ oz. Cranberry Juice
 splash Lime Juice

Chill, strain and garnish with a lime wedge.

CREME BRULEE MARTINI

  1 oz. Stoli Vanil Vodka
  1 oz. Kahlua
  3 oz. Half & Half

Shake and strain into chilled martini
glass. Garnish with light sprinkle of
sweet ground powdered cocoa.

CREOLE MARTINI

    1½ to 2 oz. Vodka
    dash Dry Vermouth, or to taste
    large Jalapeño Pepper

Mix the Vodka and Vermouth in a
shaker with ice. Strain the drink into
a chilled cocktail glass. Garnish with
pepper.

CROWN JEWELS

    2½ oz. Bombay Sapphire Gin
    ½ oz. Chambord

Stir 50 times and strain into pre-chilled
martini glass. Garnish with large fresh
red raspberry.

Charlie Ryder
Beverage Director and Sommelier
LaSalle Grill
South Bend, IN

CSONKA MARTINI

        Absolut and Chambord

Garnish with Godiva Raspberry
Chocolate.

Shulas No Name Lounge
Tampa, FL

CUB CAMPARI

    1 oz. Absolut Kurant Vodka
    1 oz. Campari
    $\frac{1}{2}$ oz. Grapefruit Juice
    $\frac{1}{2}$ oz. Cranberry Juice

Serve in a martini glass.

CUCUMBER MARTINI

Freshly muddled cucumber shaken with Belvedere Vodka & lemon zest.

Lot 61
New York, NY

CUPID'S BOW

    $\frac{1}{4}$ oz. Cork Dry Gin
    $\frac{1}{4}$ oz. Forbidden Fruit Liqueur
    $\frac{1}{4}$ oz. Curacao
    $\frac{1}{4}$ oz. Passion Fruit Juice

Shake.

CURIOUS GEORGE MARTINI

    $1\frac{1}{2}$ oz. Smirnoff Vodka
    splash Banana Liqueur
    shot Cranberry Juice

Chill, strain and garnish with a fresh banana wedge.

CZAR

 2 oz. Stoli Vodka
 ½ oz. Chambord

Chill and strain into chilled martini glass. Serve with lemon twist.

Robert Gayle
Whispers Pub
Oviedo, FL

CZARINA MARTINI

 1 oz. Smirnoff Black Vodka
 splash Dry Vermouth
 splash Apricot Brandy
 dash Bitters

Chill and strain into a martini glass.

CZAR'S STRAWBERRY CUP MARTINI

Stoli Razberi Vodka and a splash of Godet White Chocolate Liqueur chilled.

DAMN THE WEATHER MARTINI

 1½ oz. Gin
 ½ oz. Sweet Vermouth
 ½ oz. Fresh Orange Juice
 1 tsp. Triple Sec

Shake ingredients with ice. Strain into chilled glass.

DAMN THE WEATHER MARTINI II

2 oz. Finlandia Vodka
⅓ oz. Veuve Clicquot Champagne
¼ oz. Chambord

Fill mixing glass with ice, add Finlandia and Chambord. Stir well and strain into martini glass. Top with Veuve Clicquot.

Windows on the World
New York, NY

DARK CHOCOLATE MARTINI

2 oz. Smirnoff Vodka
splash Dark Creme de Cacao

Rub fresh mint leaf around the rim of the martini glass. Chill, strain and garnish with a mint leaf.

DARK CRYSTAL

2½ oz. Stolichnaya Cristall Vodka
splash Remy Martin VSOP

Stir with ice and strain. Garnish with lemon twist.

Compass Rose
San Francisco, CA

DEAN MARTINI

2 oz. Ketel One Vodka, chilled
A Lucky (cigarette) and a
book of matches

Pour the Vodka into a cocktail glass and garnish with an olive. Place the cigarette and matches on the side.

DEAN'S MARTINI

Skyy Vodka
splash Cointreau
Cranberry Juice and
Sweet and Sour Mix

Serve up in an oversized chilled stem. Shaken, not stirred.

DECADENT MARTINI

1½ oz. Smirnoff Vodka
float DiSaronno Amaretto
splash Raspberry Liqueur

Chill, strain and garnish with a chocolate kiss.

DEEP SEA MARTINI

    1½ oz. Gin
    1 oz. Dry Vermouth
   1 dash Orange Bitters
    ¼ oz. Pernod
Garnish with a twist of lemon peel.

DEITRICH MARTINI

    2 oz. Smirnoff Vodka
  splash Campari
  splash Dry Vermouth
Strain and garnish with an orange peel.

DELIVERANCE-TINI

       Jack Daniel's Black
       Fresh Lemon Juice
Serve in sugar-rimmed glass.
The Diner on Sycamore
Cincinnati, OH

DELMONICO MARTINI

    1 oz. Dry Gin
    1/2 oz. Dry Vermouth
    1/2 oz. Sweet Vermouth
    1/2 oz. Cognac
    1 dash Angostura Bitters
          Orange peel

DENISE'S MARTINI

    1 oz. Extra Dry Gin
    1 tsp. Extra Dry Vermouth
    1 small drop Red Food Dye
Shake with chipped ice. Strain into
martini glass. Add 1 extremely large
green olive. Dash of olive juice.
Denise Nalysnyk
Carpentersville, IL

DEPTH CHARGE MARTINI

    1 1/4 oz. Gin
    1 1/4 oz. Lillet
    1/4 oz. Pernod
          Orange peel

DERBY MARTINI

       Belvedere Vodka
       Dry Vermouth
  1 Olive

Served straight up or on the rocks.
Hollywood Brown Derby
Walt Disney World, FL

DERNIER ROUND MARTINI

  $1\frac{1}{2}$ oz. Dry Gin
    $\frac{1}{2}$ oz. Vermouth
    $\frac{1}{4}$ oz. Cognac
    $\frac{1}{4}$ oz. Cointreau
  1 dash Angostura Bitters

DESERT SUNSET MARTINI

  1 oz. Stoli Razberi Vodka
  1 oz. Stoli Ohranj Vodka
  splash Cointreau
  splash Orange Juice
  dash Rose's Lime Juice

Top with a dash of Grenadine for sunset
color.

DEWEY MARTINI

1½ oz. Absolut Vodka
dash Martini & Rossi Extra Dry
Vermouth
dash Orange Bitters

Shake and strain into a cocktail glass or serve over ice.

DIABLO MARTINI

1½ oz. White Port
1 oz. Dry Vermouth
¼ tsp. Fresh Lemon Juice

Shake with ice. Strain into chilled glass. Garnish with lemon twist.

DIAMOND HEAD MARTINI

1½ oz. Gin
½ oz. Orange Curacao or Triple Sec
2 oz. Pineapple Juice
1 tsp. Sweet Vermouth

Shake, strain and serve with a pineapple wedge.

DIAMONDS ARE FOREVER
   2$\frac{1}{2}$ oz. Bombay Sapphire Gin
      splash Scotch
Pour Gin and Scotch over ice and stir.
Strain into a well chilled martini glass.
Garnish with olives.
Gerard Lounge
The Sutton Place Hotel
Vancouver, BC

DIANA MARTINI
   1$\frac{1}{2}$ oz. Gin
   $\frac{3}{4}$ oz. Dry Vermouth
   $\frac{1}{4}$ oz. Sweet Vermouth
   $\frac{1}{4}$ oz. Pernod
Garnish with a twist of lemon.

DICK ST. CLAIRE'S
         Ketel One Vodka
         Cherry Heering
Freshly squeezed orange and lime
juices.

DIEGO MARTINI

 2 oz. Smirnoff Vodka
 splash Jose Cuervo Gold Tequila
 dash Orange Juice

Chill, strain and garnish with an orange wheel.

DILLATINI MARTINI

 1½ oz. Absolut Vodka
 dash Martini & Rossi Extra Dry
   Vermouth
   Dilly bean (if you can
   find one)

Shake and strain or serve over ice.

DIPLOMAT MARTINI

 1½ oz. Dry Vermouth
 ½ oz. Sweet Vermouth
 ½ tsp. Maraschino Cherry Juice
 2 dashes Angostura Bitters
   Lemon twist
   Maraschino Cherry

Shake with ice and strain into chilled glass. Garnish with lemon twist and maraschino cherry.

DIRTY MARTINI
    1½ oz. Bombay Sapphire Gin
    1¾ oz. Extra Dry Vermouth
    1 tsp. Olive Brine
           Stuffed Green Olive
Rub glass rim with lemon twist before pouring. Garnish with olive.

DIRTY SICILIAN MARTINI
           Vodka
Garnish with Colossal Sicilian Olives marinated in Vermouth and some olive brine.

DIXIE MARTINI
    2 oz. Dry Gin
    ¼ oz. Dry Vermouth
    ¼ oz. Pernod

DOG BITES BACK
    1 oz. Skyy Vodka
    1½ oz. Bloody Mary Mix
Stir with ice and strain into a chilled martini glass. Garnish with olives and lemon twist.
The Martini Club
Atlanta, GA

"BONG...BONG...BONG...BONG...
BONG...BONG...BONG!"

DON SHULA MARTINI

Belvedere Vodka served straight up.
Garnish with cocktail mushrooms.
Shulas No Name Lounge
Tampa, FL

DOVE SPECIAL

    1 oz. Stoli Cristall Vodka
    1 oz. Alizé
        1 Orange twist
Matt Hoy
Sweetwaters Restaurant
Eau Claire, WI

DOYLE'S DUBLIN MARTINI (BOSTON STYLE)

Fill pint glass with ice cubes. Pour
$1/2$ oz. Dry Vermouth. Add $2\frac{1}{2}$ oz. of
Jameson Irish Whiskey and stir. Strain
into chilled martini glass. 3 Leprechaun
size drops of Irish Mist. Slice from the
rind of a lime as green as a field of
Shamrocks.
Eddie Doyle
Bull & Finch Pub
Boston, MA

DR. MONAHAN

     2 oz. Dry Gin
     1/4 oz. Pernod
     1 dash Orange Bitters
            Lemon twist

DRAGON'S BREATH

     2 oz. Bombay Sapphire Gin
     splash Vermouth
     1/4 oz. Cointreau, flamed and
            poured into a glass
     1/4 Blood Orange squeezed
     wedge Clementine as garnish
900 West in the Hotel Vancouver
Vancouver, BC

DRESSED TO "K"ILL

     2 oz. Ketel One Vodka
     splash Grand Marnier
     splash Orange Curacao and
            Blue Curacao
Pour into mixing glass, add ice and
shake well. Splash of soda. Garnish with
orange twist and maraschino cherry.
Serve in chilled martini glass.
Ric Storozuk
Northfield Ctr., OH

DRIEST MARTINI
    1 oz. Absolut Vodka
    1 oz. Tanqueray Gin
Stir and pour into prechilled cocktail
glass. Add chunk of dry ice.
Brian Rea
Grass Valley, CA

DRY GEM
      Bombay Sapphire Gin
    dash Dry Vermouth
Black olive garnish.
Renaissance Atlanta Hotel
Atlanta, GA

DRY MARTINI (5-1)
    1⅔ oz. Gin
    ⅓ oz. Dry Vermouth
Stir Vermouth and Gin over ice cubes in
mixing glass. Strain into cocktail glass.
Serve with a twist of lemon peel or olive.

DRY MARTINI
    2 oz. Dry Gin
    splash Dry Vermouth
Garnish with a green olive or twist.
Shake or stir with ice, strain. Serve
straight up.

DRY MARTINI, WILSON'S WAY

Chill martini glass. Add dash of Dry Vermouth. Swish around and dump the excess Vermouth. Strain in glass and add 2 olives to garnish.

Wilson Aguayo
Flamingo Hotel & Casino
Bullhead City, AZ

DRY VICTORIA MARTINI

3 oz.	Bombay Sapphire Gin
1 oz.	Martini & Rossi Extra Dry Vermouth
1 or 2	dashes Orange Bitters (or orange peel)

Garnish with 1 cocktail olive and twist of lemon. Shake or stir. Serve in classic martini glass.

DU BARRY COCKTAIL MARTINI

1½ oz.	Dry Gin
¾ oz.	Dry Vermouth
¼ oz.	Pernod
1 dash	Angostura Bitters

Garnish with an orange slice.

DUBONNET COCKTAIL
MARTINI

    1 oz. Dubonnet Rouge
    1 oz. Gin
 1 dash Orange Bitters
         Lemon twist

Stir with ice and strain into chilled glass. Drop in lemon twist.

DUTCH KETEL

         Ketel One Vodka
         Tomolives

Morton's of Chicago
Washington, DC

DUSTY MARTINI

    2 oz. Smirnoff Vodka chilled

Pour several drops of J&B Scotch into the bottom of a martini glass, stir to coat. Shake out extra Scotch from the glass. Strain Vodka into the martini glass. Garnish with an olive.

DUTCH CHOCOLATE MARTINI

    2 oz. Leyden Gin
  1½ oz. Creme de Cacao
   ½ oz. Lemon Juice
   ½ tsp. Grenadine

Shake with ice and strain into cocktail glass.

Joe Nacci, Beverage Manager/Bartender
Gibson's Restaurant
Chicago, IL

EASY LIKE SUNDAY MORNING

  1½ oz. Grey Goose Vodka
    1 oz. Cointreau
   ½ oz. Passion Fruit Sorbet

Shake and float Champagne on top.
Serve with Chambord on rim of glass.

Robert Crane and Pamela Friedman
Mistral
Boston, MA

EDEN MARTINI

  1½ oz. Smirnoff Vodka
  splash Apple Liqueur

Strain and garnish with fresh apple wedge and a cinnamon stick.

EGYPTIAN CLUB CHOCOLATE MARTINI

    1 oz. Absolut Vodka
    1 oz. Truffles Dark Chocolate
            Liqueur
  1/2 oz. Baileys Irish Cream

Mix ingredients into shaker with ice. Shake and strain into chilled martini glass. Garnish with chocolate covered maraschino cherry.

Kimberly Davis
The Egyptian Club
Portland, OR

EL MARTINI PATRON

Patron Añejo served in chilled martini glass with a hint of Triple Sec and lime.

Hurricane Restaurant
Passagrille, FL

EL PRESIDENTE MARTINI

  1 1/2 oz. Tequila
   3/4 oz. Dry Vermouth
  1 dash Angostura Bitters

Stir ingredients with ice. Strain into chilled glass.

ELECTRIC PEACH MARTINI

Finlandia Vodka, chilled

¼ oz. Peach Schnapps

½ oz. Cranberry Juice Cocktail

¼ oz. Orange Juice

Finlandia Vodka Americas, Inc.
New York, NY

ELEGANT MARTINI (VODKA)

1½ oz. Absolut Vodka

dash Martini & Rossi Extra Dry
Vermouth

¼ oz. Grand Marnier

dash Grand Marnier

Stir the first three ingredients with ice.
Serve on ice or straight up. Float Grand
Marnier on top.

ELEPHANT'S EAR MARTINI

1 oz. Dry Gin

¾ oz. Martini & Rossi Dry
Vermouth

¾ oz. Dubonnet

Stir with ice. Serve on ice or straight up.

ELLIOTT CARVER™ MARTINI

Combine 1½ oz. Smirnoff Vodka with 1½ oz. Goldschlager Cinnamon Schnapps. Strain into martini glass.

EMERALD MARTINI

2 oz.	Bacardi Limón
splash	Martini & Rossi Extra Dry Vermouth
splash	Midori

Stir with ice. Serve on ice or straight up.

ENCHANTED MARTINI

1 oz.	Encantado Mezcal
¼ oz.	Dry Vermouth
1	Jalapeño or Habanero-Stuffed Olive

Shake over ice in martini shaker. Strain into martini glass. Skewer olive on tooth pick and add.

Mezcal Importers, Inc.
Napa, CA

ENGLEWOOD MARTINI

   1 oz. Stoli Ohranj Vodka
  splash Campari
  splash Orange Juice

Mix ingredients in shaker with ice. Pour into chilled martini glass.

Heather Puser
Hillsdale, NJ

ENOS MARTINI

  1¾ oz. Dry Gin
   ¾ oz. Dry Vermouth
   ¼ oz. Pernod

Garnish with a maraschino cherry.

ESCOBAR MARTINI

  1¾ oz. Tequila
   ¼ oz. Dry Vermouth

Garnish with a green olive.

ESPIONAGE MARTINI

  1½ oz. Smirnoff Citrus Twist Vodka
  splash White Creme de Menthe

Strain and garnish with a lemon twist.

ESPRESSO GRANDE MARTINI

Chilled Finlandia Vodka
1/2 oz. Kahlua
1/4 oz. Grand Marnier

Finlandia Fashion Martinis

ESPRESSO MARTINI

2 oz. Stoli Limonnaya Vodka
1/2 oz. Café Sport Borghetti Espresso
Liqueur

Garnish with a lemon twist.

EXPRESSO MARTINI II

Stolichnaya Kafya Vodka
splash Kahlua and Tia Maria

Garnish with coffee beans.

John Dourney
The Thirsty Turtle
Bernardsville, NJ

EXTERMINATOR MARTINI

2 oz. Smirnoff Vodka
1/2 oz. Fino Sherry

Chill and strain into martini glass.

FABULOUS MARTINI

    2 oz. Frozen Smirnoff Vodka
Chill and strain into well chilled martini glass. Top with dash of Champagne. Garnish with a purple grape.

FALLEN ANGEL MARTINI

    2 oz. Gin
    3/4 oz. Fresh Lemon or Lime Juice
    1 tsp. White Creme de Menthe
    1 dash Angostura Bitters
        Maraschino Cherry
Shake liquid ingredients with ice. Strain into chilled glass. Garnish with maraschino cherry.

FANTASIO MARTINI

    1 1/2 oz. Brandy
    3/4 oz. Dry Vermouth
    1 tsp. White Creme de Menthe
    1 tsp. Maraschino Cherry Juice
Shake ingredients with ice. Strain into chilled glass.

FARE-THEE-WELL MARTINI

1½ oz. Dry Gin
½ oz. Dry Vermouth
¼ oz. Sweet Vermouth
¼ oz. Orange Curacao

FARMER'S COCKTAIL MARTINI

1½ oz. Gin
¾ oz. Dry Vermouth
¾ oz. Sweet Vermouth
2 dashes Angostura Bitters

Stir ingredients with ice. Strain into chilled glass.

FASCINATOR MARTINI

1½ oz. Absolut Vodka
dash Martini & Rossi Extra Dry
    Vermouth
dash Pernod and Sprig Mint

Stir and serve straight up or over ice. Garnish with a mint sprig.

FAUX MINT JULEP

Small bag of fresh mint sprigs. Throw them in back of fridge and forget them. Pour Maker's Mark over ice. Drink, Happy Derby.

FAVORITE COCKTAIL

  ¾ oz. Gin
  ¾ oz. Dry Vermouth
  ¾ oz. Apricot Brandy
  ¼ tsp. Fresh Lemon Juice

Shake ingredients with ice. Strain into chilled glass over ice cubes.

FEENEY MARTINI

  1 part Stoli Razberi Vodka
  1 part Godiva Chocolate
        (white or dark)
  1 part Creme de Cacao
        (white or dark)

Shake and strain into chilled martini glass. Garnish with a strawberry or a chocolate kiss.

L'Opera
Long Beach, CA

FERNET BRANCA COCKTAIL MARTINI

  1½ oz. Dry Gin
  ¼ oz. Sweet Vermouth
  ½ oz. Fernet Branca

Garnish with a maraschino cherry.

FERRARI MARTINI

    2 oz. Dry Vermouth
    1 oz. Amaretto
          Lemon twist

Pour Vermouth and Amaretto into chilled glass, filled with ice cubes; stir well. Garnish with lemon twist.

FIBBER McGEE MARTINI

    2 oz. Dry Gin
    1 oz. Fresh Grapefruit Juice
    1 oz. Rosso Vermouth
 3 dashes Angostura

Shake and strain.

FIFTH AVENUE MARTINI

    $1\frac{1}{2}$ oz. Dry Gin
    $\frac{1}{2}$ oz. Dry Vermouth
    $\frac{1}{2}$ oz. Fernet Branca

FIN DE SIECLE COCKTAIL MARTINI

    $1\frac{1}{2}$ oz. Dry Gin
    $\frac{3}{4}$ oz. Sweet Vermouth
    $\frac{1}{4}$ oz. Amer Picon
    1 dash Orange Bitters

"CAN YOU PUT TOGETHER SOME MORE
OF THAT MARTINI CONCOCTION,
THAT MAKES ME A MERRY OL' SOUL."

FINAL APPROACH

    1 part Ron Rico Rum
    1 part Vermouth
Garnish with a twist of lemon.
The Windsock Bar & Grill
San Diego, CA

FINE AND DANDY
MARTINI

    $1\frac{1}{2}$ oz. Gin
    $\frac{1}{2}$ oz. Triple Sec or Cointreau
    $\frac{1}{2}$ oz. Fresh Lemon Juice
    1 dash Angostura Bitters
              Maraschino Cherry

FINLANDIA BLUE MOON

    3 parts Classic Finlandia Vodka
    3 parts Pineapple Juice
    1 part Blue Curacao Liqueur
Garnish with orange zest.

FINLANDIA CRANBERRY MARTINI

Chill martini glass with ice and
½ oz. Martini & Rossi Extra Dry
Vermouth. Stir and chill in mixing glass
2 oz. Finlandia Cranberry Vodka.
Empty martini glass of all ingredients.
Pour and strain Vodka into the freshly
chilled martini glass. Garnish with twist
of lemon.

Don Harris
E-mail

FINLANDIA GOLD DIGGER MARTINI

5 parts Classic Finlandia Vodka
1 part Pineapple Juice
2 parts Cointreau

FINLANDIA LIME GREEN MARTINI

6 parts Finlandia Vodka
1 part Grapefruit Juice
1 part Midori Melon Liqueur

Garnish with thinly sliced lemon and
lime twists.

FINLANDIA MIDNIGHT SUN MARTINI

5 parts Finlandia Cranberry Vodka
1 part Classic Finlandia Vodka
1 part Kahlua

FINLANDIA NAKED GLACIER

7 parts Classic Finlandia Vodka
splash Peppermint Schnapps
Frost rim of martini glass with
superfine sugar.

FINLANDIA PINK DIAMOND MARTINI

3 parts Finlandia Cranberry Vodka
1 part Pineapple Juice
3 parts Classic Finlandia Vodka
1 part Peach Schnapps
Garnish with the perfect maraschino
cherry.

FINLANDIA TOPAZ

5 parts Classic Finlandia Vodka
1 part Dark Creme de Cacao
1 part Frangelico

FINLANLDIA BUFF

    5 parts Classic Finlandia Vodka
    1 part Baileys Irish Cream
    1 part Kahlua

FINO MARTINI

    2 oz. Dry Gin
    ½ oz. Fino Sherry

Garnish with a green olive or a twist of lemon.

FIRE ALARM MARTINI

    4 oz. Absolut Peppar Vodka
    2 oz. Tequila
    dash Tabasco

Mix all ingredients in shaker with ice. Pour into chilled martini glass. Garnish with jalepeño pepper.

Heather Puser
Smoke
Hillsdale, NJ

FIRE AND ICE MARTINI

In a shaker filled with ice, pour 2 oz. chilled Smirnoff Vodka. Shake and strain into martini glass. Garnish with chili pepper.

FIRE IN THE HOLE
$1\frac{1}{2}$ oz. Bacardi Light Rum
$\frac{3}{4}$ oz. Peppermint Schnapps
2-3 dashes Tabasco

FIRECRACKER MARTINI
$1\frac{1}{2}$ oz. Captain Morgan Rum
$\frac{1}{2}$ oz. Grenadine
$\frac{2}{3}$ oz. 7-UP
Fill with orange juice, Bacardi 151 float.

FIREFLY MARTINI
2 oz. Smirnoff Vodka
$\frac{3}{4}$ oz. Grapefruit Juice
dash Grenadine

FLAMINGO MARTINI
$1\frac{1}{2}$ oz. Gin
$\frac{1}{2}$ oz. Apricot Brandy
$\frac{1}{2}$ oz. Fresh Lime Juice
1 tsp. Grenadine
Shake ingredients with ice. Strain into
chilled glass.

FLOWERS AND VINES

 ¾ oz. Premium Vodka
1¼ oz. Green Chartreuse
 ¾ oz. Chambord

Dribble Chambord down side of glass
to settle at bottom.

Rebecca Gass
Blueberry Hill
St. Louis, MO

FLUFFY DUCK MARTINI

1½ oz. Dry Gin
1½ oz. Advocaat Liqueur
 1 oz. Fresh Orange Juice
 ½ oz. Cointreau

Mix and top with soda water.

FLYING BLACK TIE

 3 oz. Grey Goose Vodka
 ¼ oz. Scotch
 ¼ oz. Campari

Stir and place into tumbler with ice,
shake and serve. Garnish with toothpick
with a pearl onion in the center of two
black olives.

Nelson Souza
Astor Hotel
Miami, FL

FLYING DUTCHMAN

1¾ oz. Dry Gin
¼ oz. French Vermouth
2 dashes Orange Curacao

FLYING DUTCHMAN II

2 oz. Beefeater Gin
¼ oz. Blue Curacao

Shake over ice and strain into chilled glass.

FOGGI DAY MARTINI

Beefeater Gin
Pernod
Dry Vermouth

MAD 28
New York, NY

FORTUNELLA MARTINI

¼ oz. Campari
¾ oz. Caravella Limoncella
¼ oz. Cointreau
¾ oz. Bombay Sapphire Gin
1 oz. Ketel One Vodka
1 tsp. Candied Kumquat Nectar
1 Lemon Slice

Coat ice cold mixing glass with Campari and toss out excess. Add ingredients and ice, shake and strain into ice cold martini glass. Garnish with lemon twist and kumquat.

Four Seasons Olympic Hotel
Seattle, WA

FOUR ALARM MARTINI

4 oz. Absolut Peppar Vodka
2 oz. Tequila
dash Tabasco

Mix all ingredients in shaker with ice. Pour into chilled martini glass. Garnish with jalepeño pepper.

Heather Puser
Hillsdale, NJ

FOURTH DEGREE MARTINI

    $3/4$ oz. Dry Gin
    $3/4$ oz. Dry Vermouth
    $3/4$ oz. Sweet Vermouth
    $1/4$ oz. Pernod

Stir gently with ice. Serve straight up or over ice. Garnish with lemon peel twist.

FRAMBOISE MARTINI

    2 oz. Absolut Vodka
    $1/4$ oz. Chambord Liqueur
    1 Raspberry

San Ysidro Ranch
Santa Barbara, CA

FRANGELICO MARTINI

    $1 1/4$ oz. Absolut Vodka
    $1/4$ oz. Frangelico Liqueur
    $1/2$ oz. Tuaca Liqueur

Stir with ice and strain into a chilled martini glass.

Pravda
New York, NY

FRANK-A-TINI

Absolut Kurant Vodka
Teen-tiny touch of Sweet
Vermouth and Raspberries

No. 18
New York, NY

FRANKENJACK COCKTAIL
MARTINI

1 oz. Gin
½ oz. Dry Vermouth
½ oz. Apricot Brandy
1 tsp. Triple Sec or Cointreau
Maraschino Cherry

Shake liquid ingredients with ice. Strain
into chilled glass. Garnish with
maraschino cherry.

FREEBORN FLOATER

Ketel One Vodka
Lime Juice
Tomolives

Yvette Wintergarden
Chicago, IL

FRENCH HORN

    2½ oz. Absolut Kurant Vodka
    ½ oz. Chambord
Garnish with a lemon twist.

FRENCH KISS MARTINI

    2 oz. Stolichnaya Ohranj Vodka
    ¼ oz. Lillet
Stir gently with ice. Serve straight up or over ice.

FRENCH MARTINI

    2 oz. Smirnoff Vodka
    splash Cognac
Shake well and strain into a martini glass.

FRENCH MARTINI II
(A.K.A PAISLEY MARTINI)

    ¼ oz. Scotch Whisky
    1½ oz. Gin
Lemon twist garnish.

FROTH BLOWER COCKTAIL MARTINI

2 oz. Gin
1 Egg White
1 tsp. Grenadine

Blend and strain into chilled glass.

FRUIT BURST MARTINI

1/2 oz. Blue Curacao
1/2 oz. Vodka
1/2 oz. Vermouth
1/2 oz. Peach Schnapps
Pineapple Juice

Place into shaker quarter filled with ice.
Top with pineapple juice. Shake and
serve in shot glass.

Kevin Hare
Bedrocks Bar & Casino
Lower Hutt, New Zealand

FRUIT OF THE FOREST

Fresh summer berries shaken with
Wyborowa Lemon Vodka. Garnished
with berries.

FRUITY MARTINI

    1¼ oz. Gordon's Grapefruit Gin
    1¼ oz. Stoli Ohranj Vodka
    ½ oz. Chambord

Shake and strain into a chilled martini glass.

FUDGICLE MARTINI

        Chilled Finlandia Vodka
    ½ oz. Creme de Cacao
    ¼ oz. Chocolate Syrup

FUZZY GATOR

    2 oz. Stolichnaya Vodka
  splash Peach Schnapps
  splash Gatorade

Garnish with a long lime twist.

FUZZY MARTINI

    1½ oz. Smirnoff Vodka
    ½ oz. Peach Schnapps

Chill, strain and serve into a chilled martini glass.

FUZZY MARTINI II

    2 oz. Stoli Vanil Vodka
    1 oz. Stoli Persik Vodka
1 splash Peach Schnapps
Garnish with thin peach slice.

FUZZY NAVAL MARTINI

    2 oz. Ketel One Vodka
    $\frac{1}{2}$ oz. Peach Schnapps
    $\frac{1}{2}$ oz. Freshly Squeezed Orange Juice
Orange peel for garnish.
Ed Carlo, Bartender
Stage Left

FUZZY ZINILLA

    3 oz. Stoli Vanil Vodka
    1 oz. Stoli Zinamon Vodka
    $\frac{1}{2}$ oz. Peach Schnapps
        Orange twist
Gilbert Valentine
Larkspur Restaurant & Grill
Wichita, KS

GARDEN MARTINI

    2 oz. Smirnoff Vodka in
             shaker with
3 drops Dry Vermouth
Strain and garnish with cherry tomato
and pickled asparagus spear.

GAZETTE MARTINI

1½ oz. Brandy
¾ oz. Sweet Vermouth
1 tsp. Lemon Juice
½ tsp. Sugar
Shake with ice and strain into
chilled glass.

GENE TUNNEY MARTINI

1¾ oz. Dry Gin
¾ oz. Dry Vermouth
dash Lemon Juice
dash Orange Juice
Garnish with a maraschino cherry.

"HOLD IT, IT LOOKS LIKE
A DRY MARTINI."

GEORGE'S WAY

> Beefeater Gin
> Dry Vermouth
splash Pernod

Hamiltons
Miami, Fl

GEORGETOWN MARTINI

> Ketel One Vodka
splash Grand Marnier
> Orange Slice

Morton's "Martini Club"

GEORGIA PEACH

1 oz. Ketel One Vodka
½ oz. Peach Schnapps
1 oz. Orange Juice

Stir with ice and strain into a chilled
martini glass. Garnish with peach slice.

The Martini Club
Atlanta, GA

GIBSON MARTINI

2½ oz. Dry Gin
splash French Vermouth

Garnish with an onion.

GILROY MARTINI

    1 oz. Gin
    1 oz. Cherry Brandy
    ½ oz. Dry Vermouth
    ½ oz. Fresh Lemon Juice
4 dashes Orange Bitters

Shake ingredients with ice. Strain into chilled glass.

GIMLET MARTINI

    1½ oz. Bombay Gin
    dash Rose's Lime Juice

Stir in cocktail glass. Strain & serve straight up or on the rocks. Garnish with lime.

GIN 'N' IT MARTINI

    1½ oz. Dry Gin
    ½ oz. Italian Vermouth

Garnish with a twist of lemon

GIN ALOHA MARTINI

   1½ oz. Gin
   1½ oz. Triple Sec
   ½ oz. Unsweetened Pineapple Juice
 2 dashes Orange Bitters

Shake ingredients with ice. Strain into chilled glass.

GIN AND SIN

   1½ oz. Beefeater Gin
   ¾ oz. Lemon Juice
   ½ oz. Orange Juice
  dashes Grenadine
       1 Barspoon Powdered Sugar
         Stemmed Maraschino Cherry

Shake well over ice cubes in a shaker. Strain into cocktail glass or serve over ice. Add maraschino cherry.

GIN COCKTAIL

   2 oz. Gin
 2 dashes Orange Bitters
         Lemon twist

Stir liquid ingredients with ice. Strain into chilled glass. Drop in lemon twist.

GIN CRUSTA MARTINI

    2 oz. Dry Gin
    ½ oz. Lemon Juice
    ½ oz. Cointreau
    tsp. Maraschino Cherry Juice
    dash Angostura

Shake, and strain into prepared glass.

GINGER MARTINI

Freshly muddled Ginger shaken with a large pour of Skyy Vodka. Orange zest and a dash of sugar.

GIN RUSH MARTINI

    4½ oz. Leyden Gin
  3 dashes Angostura Bitters
    ½ oz. Triple Sec

Mix all ingredients with cracked ice in a shaker. Strain into chilled cocktail glass. Serve with lemon twist.

Joe Nacci, Beverage Manager/Bartender
Gibson's Restaurant
Chicago, IL

GINSATIONAL MARTINI

1½ oz. Schlichte Steinhaeger Gin
¼ oz. Dry Vermouth
Garnish with a twist of lemon, and
an olive.

GINSENG MARTINI

1 American Ginseng root
1 bottle Vodka
Let stand for two days. Splash of Dry
Vermouth. Ginger slice for garnish.
Le Colonial
West Hollywood, CA

GIN SIDECAR MARTINI

2 oz. Dry Gin
1 oz. Lemon Juice
1 oz. Cointreau
Shake and strain.

GINA'S CHOCOLATE RASPBERRY MARTINI

      Belvedere Vodka
      White Chocolate Liqueur
      Dark Chocolate Liqueur
      Martini & Rossi Rosso
      Vermouth
      Raspberry Liqueur

Garnish with a fresh raspberry marinated in Vodka.

Rhumba
Chicago, IL

GIN-CASSIS MARTINI

  2 oz. Dry Gin
1½ oz. Creme de Cassis
  1 tsp. Lemon Juice

Shake and strain.

GINKA MARTINI

1¼ oz. Dry Gin
1¼ oz. Vodka
½ oz. Dry Vermouth

Garnish with a lemon peel or a green olive.

GINWIN MARTINI

    1 oz. Absolut Kurant Vodka
    1 oz. Absolut Citron Vodka
    ¼ oz. Grand Marnier
Garnish with twist.
Jason Bowers
Regas
Knoxville, TN

GLACIER BLUE MARTINI

    Stolichnaya Vodka
    Bombay Gin
    Blue Curacao
Oliver's Mayflower Park Hotel
Seattle, WA

GLACIER MINT MARTINI

Combine 2 oz. Smirnoff Vodka with
½ oz. Peppermint Schnapps. Strain into
chilled martini glass.

GLAMOUROUS MARTINI

    2 oz. Smirnoff Vodka
    dash Orange Juice
    dash Grapefruit Juice
    splash Orange Liqueur
Chill, strain, garnish with an orange wheel.

GLOBAL TIME

    1 part Tanqueray Gin
   splash Chambord
          Lemon twist

The Windsock Bar & Grill
San Diego, CA

GLOOM CHASER MARTINI

   1½ oz. Dry Gin
    ½ oz. French Vermouth
 2 dashes Pernod
 2 dashes Grenadine

GODIVA APRICOT MARTINI

    1 part Godiva Liqueur
    1 part Absolut Vodka
    1 part Apricot Brandy

Combine with ice, shake well. Serve
chilled with maraschino cherry.

The House of Seagram
New York, NY

GODIVA BLACK CURRANT MARTINI

    1 oz. Godiva Liqueur
    1 oz. Seagram's Gin
    $1/4$ oz. Creme de Cassis
    $1/6$ oz. Lemon Juice
    $1/6$ oz. Lime Juice

Combine with ice; shake well. Service chilled. Garnish with maraschino cherry.

GODIVA CRANBERRY MARTINI

    1 part Godiva Liqueur
    1 part Absolut Vodka
    1 part Cranberry Juice

Combine with ice; shake well. Serve chilled. Garnish with lime twist.

The House of Seagram
New York, NY

GODIVA MANDARIN MARTINI

    1 part Godiva Liqueur
    1 part Absolut Vodka
    splash Cointreau or orange juice

Combine with ice; shake well. Serve chilled. Garnish with orange slice.

GODIVA MINT MARTINI

    1 part Godiva Liqueur
    1 part Absolut Vodka
    splash White Creme de Menthe

Combine with ice; shake well. Serve chilled. Garnish with mint leaf.

The House of Seagram
New York, NY

GODIVA NAKED MARTINI

    1 part Godiva Liqueur
    1 part Absolut Vodka

Combine with ice; shake well. Serve chilled. Garnish with lemon peel or strawberry.

The House of Seagram
New York, NY

GODIVA NUTTY MARTINI

    1 part Godiva Liqueur
    1 part Absolut Vodka
    splash Frangelico or Amaretto
              Liqueur

Combine with ice; shake well. Serve chilled. Garnish with three almonds.

The House of Seagram
New York, NY

GODIVA RASPBERRY MARTINI

    1 part Godiva Liqueur
    1 part Absolut Vodka
    splash Chambord or Raspberry
            Liqueur

Combine with ice; shake well. Served chilled. Garnish with powdered sugar glass rim.

The House of Seagram
New York, NY

GODSPEED GLENN MARTINI

    3 oz. Bombay Sapphire Gin
    splash Noilly Prat Vermouth
    splash Olive Juice

Shake well with ice. Garnish with olive, twist of lemon & onion on a toothpick.

Renaissance Mayflower Hotel
Washington, DC

GOLD DIGGER MARTINI

    1 oz. Finlandia Vodka
    ½ oz. Cointreau
    ½ oz. Pineapple Juice

Stir with ice; serve straight up or over ice.

GOLDFINGER

    2 oz. Belvedere Vodka
    1/2 oz. Cointreau
       1 Orange Slice
    1/8 tsp. Edible gold dust

Pour Vodka and Cointreau over ice in a
Boston shaker. Stir in gold dust and
squeeze orange slice before adding to
shaker. Shake and strain into a well
chilled martini glass. Garnish with
orange peel.

Gerard Lounge
The Sutton Place Hotel
Vancouver, BC

GOLD MARTINI

    Stolichnaya Vodka
    Goldschlager Cinnamon Schnapps
    Lemon twist

No. 18
New York, NY

GOLDEN GIRL MARTINI

    1 3/4 oz. Beefeater Gin
    3/4 oz. Dry Sherry
    1 dash Orange Bitters
    1 dash Angostura Bitters

GOLDEN GOOSE

    1½ oz. Grey Goose Vodka
    ½ oz. Grand Marnier
    splash OJ

Shake with ice vigorously to make ice crystals form. Strain and pour into frozen 'tini' glass & serve with a zest of orange.

Julie Grant
Puzzles
Atlanta, GA

GOLDEN MARTINI

    7 parts Gordon's Gin
    1 part French Vermouth

Twist of lemon peel.

GOLDEN NUGGET MARTINI

    2 oz. Smirnoff Vodka
    dash Hazelnut Liqueur

Chill, strain and sprinkle with lightly roasted pine nuts.

GOLF MARTINI
$1\frac{3}{4}$ oz. Dry Gin
$\frac{3}{4}$ oz. Dry Vermouth
2 dashes Angostura Bitters

GOOSE BERRY
$1\frac{1}{2}$ oz. Grey Goose Vodka
1 oz. Godiva White Chocolate
Liqueur
$\frac{1}{2}$ oz. Chambord
Shake with ice and strain into chilled
martini glass. Garnish with three
raspberries.
Jason Smith
Tavern on Rush
Chicago, IL

GOOSE BERRY II
3 parts Grey Goose Vodka
1 part Triple Sec
1 part Peach Schnapps
Squeeze Fresh Lime
Garnish with floating rose petals.
Brendan Card and Jose Carson
The Bubble Lounge
San Francisco, CA

GOOSE D'ETAT MARTINI

Fill shaker with ice.

   3½ oz. Grey Goose Vodka
   ¾ oz. Lillet

Shake vigorously. Strain into chilled
glass. Garnish with brie stuffed
black olive.

Joseph E. Moorhead
Blackhawk Lodge
Chicago, IL

GOOSE THE MONK MARTINI

   3 oz. Grey Goose Vodka
   drop Chartreuse

Shake over ice and strain. Serve with
a twist.

Robert Sturdevant
Capital Grille
Boston, MA

GORDON'S CONTINENTAL MARTINI

        Gordon's Vodka
        Ghost of Dry Vermouth
        Lemon stuffed olive

"I'LL HAVE A GIN MARTINI AND HOLD
THE OLIVE. I'M ON A DIET!"

GORDON'S CUP MARTINI

    2 oz. Gordon's Dry Gin
    2 oz. Port Wine

Pour on-the-rocks in tall glass. Top with
7-Up or fizzy lemonade. Garnish with
rounds of lemon and cucumber. Sprig
of mint in season.

GORDON'S PARADISE MARTINI

    2 parts Gordon's Orange Vodka
    1 part Orange Juice

Shake with ice and pour into martini
glass. Garnish with orange slice.

GORDON'S POWER MARTINI

    1½ oz. Gordon's Orange Vodka
    ½ oz. Lemon Juice
    3 oz. Orange Juice
    1 oz. Raspberry Syrup

Pour ingredients into mixing glass. Add
ice, shake well and strain into chilled
martini glass. Garnish with orange peel.

GOTHAM

Smirnoff Black
dash Campari

Garnished with a trio of olives.

GRAN MARTINI

Fill mixing glass to top with ice. Add $1/3$
shot Grand Marnier. Add $3^1/2$ oz. of
your favorite Vodka. Strain into chilled
martini glass. Garnish with lemon or
orange twist.

Bob Phillips
Messina's @ the Crossroads
E-mail

GRAND CRANTINI

2 oz. Chilled Finlandia Arctic
Cranberry Vodka

GRAND MARTINI

$1^1/2$ oz. Smirnoff Vodka
splash Orange Liqueur
splash Orange Juice

Chill, strain and garnish with an
orange peel.

GRAND MARTINI II
    Stolichnaya Cristall Vodka
    Light dash of Grand Marnier
Garnish with orange twist.
Renaissance Atlanta Hotel
Atlanta, GA

GRAND OBSESSION
    Absolut Kurant Vodka
    Grand Marnier
splash Cranberry Juice

GRAND VODKA MARTINI
2$\frac{1}{4}$ oz. Ketel One Vodka
$\frac{1}{4}$ oz. Grand Marnier
Stir with ice and strain into a chilled
martini glass. Garnish with orange slice.
The Martini Club
Atlanta, GA

GRANNY GOOSE
    Grey Goose Vodka
splash Grand Marnier
Garnish with an orange twist.
Jim Jordan
Blue Light Café
San Francisco, CA

GRAPPA MARTINI

        Stoli Vodka
        Grappa Di Moscato

Garnish with olives.

Tunnel Bar Raphael
Providence, RI

GREAT SECRET MARTINI

1¾ oz. Dry Gin
 ¾ oz. Lillet
   dash Angostura Bitters

Garnish with an orange peel.

GREEN HORNET MARTINI

        Chilled Finlandia Vodka
¼ oz. Midori
½ oz. Sweet & Sour Mix

GREEN LANTERN MARTINI

 ¼ oz. Midori
 ¼ oz. Lime Juice
1½ oz. Vodka
1 twist Lemon

Blend & stir.

GREEN MARTINI

   1¼ oz. Stoli Ohranj Vodka

3 splashes Extra Dry Vermouth

   ½ oz. Midori

Combine in shaker with ice. Shake well
and strain into martini glass. Garnish
with twist of lemon.

Jane Lomshek, Bartender
Holidome
Lawrence, KS

GREEN ROOM MARTINI

   1½ oz. Dry Vermouth

   ½ oz. Brandy

  2 drops Cointreau

         Orange twist

Shake liquid ingredients with ice. Strain
into chilled glass. Drop in orange twist.

GREENBRIER MARTINI

   1 oz. Dry Gin

   ½ oz. Italian Vermouth

Garnish with a sprig of mint and a
lemon twist.

GREY GOOSE A L'ORANGE MARTINI

 4 oz. Grey Goose Vodka
 1 oz. Cointreau
 splash Campari
 splash Peach Schnapps

Flute
New York, NY

GREY GOOSE PASSION

 3 oz. Grey Goose Vodka
 1 dash Dry Vermouth
 ½ oz. Fresh Passion Fruit Puree

Combine ingredients in mixing glass. Stir gently. Strain into a chilled martini glass.

Albert Trummer
Danube Restaurant & Bar
New York, NY

GUARDS MARTINI

 1¾ oz. Dry Gin
 ¾ oz. Sweet Vermouth
 ¼ oz. Orange Curacao

Garnish with an orange peel or a maraschino cherry.

GUMDROP MARTINI

Sugar rim of Martini glass

2 oz.	Bacardi Limón
1 oz.	Belvedere Vodka
½ oz.	Southern Comfort
½ oz.	Sweet and Sour Mix
	Mist of Martini & Rossi Extra Dry Vermouth

Shake vigorously. Garnish with your choice of three tricolored gumdrops, and a sugared lemon wheel.

Magnums
Chicago, IL

GUNGA DIN MARTINI

3 parts	Dry Gin
1 part	Dry Vermouth
	Juice of ¼ Orange

Shake with ice. Garnish with a pineapple slice.

GYPSY COCKTAIL MARTINI
    1½ oz. Gin
      1 oz. Sweet Vermouth
             Maraschino Cherry
Stir liquid ingredients with ice. Strain into chilled glass. Garnish with maraschino cherry.

GYPSY MARTINI
    1½ oz. Bombay Gin
     dash Martini & Rossi Extra Dry
             Vermouth
Stir in cocktail glass. Strain & serve straight up or on the rocks. Add maraschino cherry.

H AND H MARTINI
    1¾ oz. Dry Gin
     ¾ oz. Lillet
     ¼ oz. Orange Curacao
Orange peel garnish.

H.P.W. MARTINI
     2 oz. Dry Gin
     ¼ oz. French Vermouth
     ¼ oz. Italian Vermouth
Orange peel garnish.

HAKAM MARTINI

    1¼ oz. Dry Gin
    1¼ oz. Sweet Vermouth
    ¼ oz. Orange Curacao
    1 dash Orange Bitters
           Maraschino Cherry

HALF & HALF MARTINI

    3 parts Bombay Gin
    3 parts Stolichnaya Vodka
    1 part Dry Vermouth
Garnish with lemon twist.

HALF AND HALF
(FRENCH KISS)

    1 part Martini & Rossi Sweet
           Vermouth
    1 part Martini & Rossi Dry
           Vermouth
Serve on the rocks and stir well.
Garnish with twist of orange or lemon.

HAMLET'S MARTINI
    1 oz. Iced Vodka
    1 oz. Iced Gin
    splash Dry Vermouth
Garnish with cocktail onion on a sword.

HANALEI BLUE MARTINI
       Pineapple infused Skyy Vodka
       Blue Curacao
Serve up in an oversized chilled stem.
Shaken, not stirred.
Skyy Martini List

HANKY PANKY MARTINI
    1¾ oz. Dry Gin
    ¾ oz. Sweet Vermouth
    ¼ oz. Fernet Branca
       Orange Peel

HARIKIDITINI
    1½ oz. Shochu
    splash Dry Saki
Shake and strain. Garnish with ume.
Alan Hara
E-mail

HAROLD'S MARTINI

(for those who never have more
than one!)

    4 oz. Dry Gin
    ½ oz. French Vermouth
    1 dash Orange Bitters

Stir and pour into a 6-oz. carafe. Bury the
carafe in shaved ice and serve with a frosted cocktail glass and a stuffed green olive.

John F. Pfluhg
E-mail

HARRY'S MARTINI

    1¾ oz. Dry Gin
    ¾ oz. Sweet Vermouth
    ¼ oz. Pernod

Stir gently with ice. Serve straight up or
on ice. Garnish with mint sprigs.

HARRY'S MARTINI
(San Francisco Style)

    2 oz. Bombay Gin
    ¼ oz. Green Chartreuse

Shake with ice and strain into chilled
martini glass. Garnish with lemon twist.

Harry Denton's Starlight Room
San Francisco, CA

HASTY COCKTAIL
   1¼ oz. Dry Gin
   ¾ oz. Dry Vermouth
   ¼ oz. Grenadine
   1 dash Pernod

HAVANA CLUB MARTINI
   1½ oz. Light Rum
   ½ oz. Dry Vermouth
Shake ingredients with crushed ice.
Strain into chilled glass.

HAVANA MARTINI
      Ocumare White Rum
   dash Mango Passion
Hamiltons
Miami, FL

HAWAIIAN COCKTAIL MARTINI
   2 oz. Gin
   ½ oz. Triple Sec
   ½ oz. Unsweetened Pineapple Juice
Shake ingredients with ice. Strain into
chilled glass.

HAWAIIAN MARTINI

   1½ oz. Gin
   ½ tsp. Dry Vermouth
   ½ tsp. Sweet Vermouth
   ½ tsp. Pineapple Juice

Mix all ingredients with cracked ice
in blender. Strain into chilled
cocktail glass.

Vania Thompson
Springfield, MO

HAZELNUT MARTINI

      Gordon's Vodka
  splash Frangelico

Add orange slice.

HENNESSY MARTINI

      Hennessey V.S.O.P.
      Lemon Juice

Shake and garnish with lemon.

HIGHLAND FLING MARTINI

- 2 oz. Scotch
- 1 oz. Sweet Vermouth
- 2 to 4 dashes Orange Bitters
- Green Olive

Shake liquid ingredients with ice.
Strain into chilled glass. Drop in olive.

HI-LIFE CAMOMILE MARTINI

- 1¼ oz. Camomile Tea infused Vodka
- ¼ oz. Honey

Garnish with lemon twist. Infuse Vodka
with fresh camomile for 24 hours. Take
desired portion of Vodka, shake and
strain into martini glass. Garnish with
honey and lemon peel.

Michel Mourachian, Manager
Kevin Clayborn, Manager
Bill Kenny, GM
HI Life
New York, NY

HILLIARD MARTINI

- 1¼ oz. Dry Gin
- ¾ oz. Sweet Vermouth
- 1 dash Peychaud's Bitters

HILLSBORO MARTINI
  1¾ oz. Dry Gin
  ¾ oz. Dry Vermouth
  1 dash Orange Bitters
  1 dash Angostura Bitters

HOFFMAN HOUSE MARTINI
  ¾ oz. Dry Gin
  ¾ oz. French Vermouth
  2 dashes Orange Bitters
      Green Olive

HOLE-IN-ONE MARTINI
  2 oz. Scotch
  ¾ oz. Dry Vermouth
  ¼ tsp. Fresh Lemon Juice
  1 dash Orange Bitters
Shake ingredients with ice. Strain into
chilled glass.

HOMESTEAD MARTINI
  1½ oz. Smirnoff Black Vodka
    dash Martini & Rossi Extra Dry
      Vermouth
Add orange slice muddled.

"I'LL HAVE ANOTHER!"

HONG KONG MARTINI

2 parts Dry Gin
1 part French Vermouth
$\frac{1}{4}$ tsp. Sugar Syrup
1 tsp. Lime Juice
1 dash Angostura Bitters

HONOLULU HURRICANE MARTINI

4 parts Dry Gin
1 part French Vermouth
1 part Italian Vermouth
1 tsp. Pineapple Juice

HOP SCOTCH

2 oz. OP.
$\frac{1}{2}$ oz. Dry Vermouth
Float Scotch on top.

HOT 'N BOTHERED MARTINI

Peachtree Schnapps
dash Hot Damn! Schnapps
splash Vodka

HOT LIPS MARTINI

        Chilled Finlandia
        Arctic Cranberry Vodka
¼ oz. Goldschlager
Finlandia Fashion Martinis

HOT POTATO

1½ oz. Glacier Vodka
  dash Vermouth
  dash Tabasco Sauce

HOT SPOT MARTINI

Equal parts Hot Damn! Schnapps.
Crantasia Schnapps, and Vodka.

HOTEL PLAZA MARTINI

1 oz. Dry Gin
¾ oz. French Vermouth
¾ oz. Italian Vermouth
Fill a glass with ice; garnish with a
pineapple spear.

HOTZINI

2 oz.	Ketel One Vodka
1	"Charleston Hots" Pepper with pin holes (may substitute a Serrano Pepper)
1 fresh	Oyster on the half-shell
¼ oz.	Oscira Caviar
1 frozen	martini glass

Place 5 to 10 holes in pepper. Chill Ketel One Vodka in a shaker glass with a pepper. Pour into frozen martini glass. Remove pepper from shaker and put in martini glass. Present glass on a small plate with oyster and caviar atop as garnish.

Charleston Place
Charleston, SC

HULA-HOOP MARTINI

	Chilled Finlandia Vodka
1 oz.	Pineapple Juice
½ oz.	Orange Juice

Finlandia Fashion Martinis

ICEBERG MARTINI

2 oz. Beefeater Gin
splash White Creme de Menthe
Stir with ice and strain. Garnish with
mint.

IDEAL MARTINI

1½ oz. Gin
1 oz. Dry Vermouth
1 tsp. Unsweetened Grapefruit Juice
4 dashes Maraschino Cherry Juice
Shake liquid ingredients with ice. Strain
into chilled glass. Garnish with
maraschino cherry.

IDONIS MARTINI

2 oz. Smirnoff Vodka
½ oz. Apricot Brandy
1 oz. Pineapple Juice
Chill, strain and garnish with a
pineapple slice.

IGUANA

        Absolut Citron Vodka
        Midori Melon Liqueur
splash Triple Sec
Lemon twist garnish.

IMPERIAL COCKTAIL MARTINI

1½ oz. Gin
1½ oz. Dry Vermouth
½ oz. Maraschino Cherry Juice
2 dashes Angostura Bitters
Stir liquid ingredients with ice. Strain into chilled glass. Garnish with maraschino cherry.

"IN AND OUT" MARTINI

2 oz. Gin or Vodka
¼ oz. Dry Vermouth
Fill shaker glass with ice and add Vermouth. Swirl ice around in glass & pour out. Add Gin/Vodka and shake vigorously. Pour into cocktail glass. Garnish with lemon twist or olive.

Patrick Ford
Smith & Wollensky's
New York, NY

INCA MARTINI

    1 oz. Gin
    ½ oz. Dry Vermouth
    ½ oz. Sweet Vermouth
    ½ oz. Dry Sherry
    1 dash Angostura Bitters
    1 dash Orgeat Syrup

Stir ingredients with ice. Strain into chilled glass.

INDIGO BLUE MARTINI

    Skyy Vodka
    Blue Curacao

Garnish with a lemon twist.
Bally's
Las Vegas, NV

INDISPENSABLE MARTINI

    1½ oz. Dry Gin
    ½ oz. French Vermouth
    ½ oz. Italian Vermouth
    ¼ oz. Pernod

INSPIRATION

    1 oz. Cork Dry Gin
    ¼ oz. Dry Vermouth
    ¼ oz. Calvados
    ¼ oz. Grand Marnier
Mix and add maraschino cherry.

INTERNATIONAL MARTINI

    4 parts Dry Gin
    1 part French Vermouth
    1 part Italian Vermouth
  2 dashes Creme de Cassis

IRIE MARTINI

    Bacardi Rum
  splash Tia Maria
  splash Grand Marnier
No. 18
New York, NY

IRISH MARTINI

Tullamore Dew Irish Whiskey and
Baileys served in cinnamon and sugar
rimmed glass.
Cecilia's
Breckenridge, CO

IRON CURTAIN KILLER KAMIKAZE

4 count Stoli Vodka
2 count Triple Sec
2 Lemon Wedges
1 Lime Wedge
splash Tonic

Add double splash of 7-Up.

Rob Styron
Scarcellas Italian Grille
Temecula, CA

ISLAND MARTINI

2 oz. Vodka (or Gin)
1/4 oz. Blue Curacao

Garnish with orange speared with umbrella.

Jill Stevens
Trabuco Canyon, CA

ITALIAN ICE MARTINI

2 oz. Smirnoff Citrus Twist Vodka
splash Sweet & Sour Mix

Pour into a glass with one ice cube and garnish with a lemon twist.

ITALIAN MARTINI

   1½ oz. Fris Vodka
      dash Hiram Walker Amaretto

ITALIAN MARTINI II

   1½ oz. Bombay Gin
      dash Hiram Walker Amaretto
Stir in cocktail glass. Strain & serve
straight up or on the rocks. Add lemon
twist or olive.

ITALIAN MARTINI III

       Belvedere Vodka
       Frangelico
Mad 28
New York, NY

ITALIAN MARTINI IV

   2 oz. Artic (Italian) Vodka
   1 oz. Campari

ITALIA-TINI

            Stoli Vodka
  splash Amaretto
Pazzaluna
Saint Paul, MN

JACK FROST MARTINI

  2 oz. Smirnoff Vodka
  float Peppermint Schnapps
Chill, strain and garnish with a
peppermint candy stick.

JACKIE O MARTINI

  1½ oz. Smirnoff Vodka
  splash Apricot Brandy
  dash Grenadine
  dash Pineapple Juice
Chill, strain and garnish with a
pineapple wedge.

JACKSON MARTINI

  1½ oz. Absolut Vodka
  dash Dubonnet
  dash Angostura Bitters
Stir with ice; serve with ice or strain.

JAMAICAN MARTINI

    2 oz. Absolut Vodka
    1/2 oz. Tia Maria
Shake. Serve up or on the rocks.

JAMES BOND MARTINI

    3 parts Gordon's Gin
    1 part Vodka
    1/2 part Lillet
Shake ingredients with ice until very
cold. Pour into a chilled glass. Then add
a large thin slice of lemon peel.

JAPANESE PEAR MARTINI

Fresh muddled pear shaken with
Belvedere Vodka & zest.
Lot 61
New York, NY

JAZZ MARTINI

        Bombay Sapphire Gin
        Lime Juice
        Creme de Cassis
MAD 28
New York, NY

JEREMIAH TOWER'S STARTINI

Rinse with Martini & Rossi
Extra Dry Vermouth
2 oz. Belvedere Vodka
few drops Edmond Briottet Mandarine
Liqueur
Stirred, not shaken
Garnish with Orange Zest.
Star's
San Francisco, CA

JERSEY LIGHTNING MARTINI

2 oz. Lairds Applejack Brandy
1 oz. Sweet Vermouth
3/4 oz. Fresh Lime Juice
Shake. Strain into chilled glass.

JET LOUNGE'S CHOCOLATE-TINI

1 1/2 oz. Ketel One Vodka
1/2 oz. White Creme de Cacao
1/2 oz. Martini & Rossi Extra Dry
Vermouth
Chocolate kiss
Reebok Sports Clubs

JEWEL COCKTAIL MARTINI

    1 oz. Gin
    ½ oz. Green Chartreuse
    ¼ oz. Sweet Vermouth
  2 dashes Orange Bitters

Shake liquid ingredients with ice. Strain into chilled glass. Garnish with maraschino cherry.

JEWEL MARTINI

  1½ oz. Bacardi Limón
          Emerald – splash of Midori
          Sapphire – splash of
          Blue Curacao
          Ruby – splash of
          Cranberry Juice

Gatsby
Boca Raton, FL

JOCKEY CLUB MARTINI

  1½ oz. Gin
    2 tsp. Fresh Lemon Juice
    ¼ tsp. White Creme de Cacao
    1 dash Angostura Bitters

Shake ingredients with ice. Strain into chilled glass.

JOURNALIST MARTINI

   1½ oz. Dry Gin
   ¼ oz. Sweet Vermouth
   ¼ oz. Dry Vermouth
  1 dash Angostura Bitters
  1 dash Lemon Juice
  1 dash Orange Curacao

JOY JUMPER MARTINI

  1½ oz. Smirnoff Vodka
   2 tsp. Kummel
  splash Lime Juice
  splash Lemon Juice
   dash Sugar

Chill, strain and garnish with a lemon twist.

JUDGETTE COCKTAIL MARTINI

  1 oz. Gin
  ¾ oz. Dry Vermouth
  ¾ oz. Peach Brandy
  1 tsp. Fresh Lime Juice

Shake liquid ingredients with ice. Strain into chilled glass. Garnish with maraschino cherry.

JUMPIN' JIVE MARTINI

 1 1/2 oz. Smirnoff Citrus Vodka
  1 oz. Pear Liqueur
  dash Peach Schnapps
 splash Cranberry and Lime Juice

Garnish slice pear. Shake and strain.

Brendan Lee
Richards on Richards
Vancouver, BC

JUNGLE MARTINI

  1 oz. Dry Gin
  3/4 oz. Sweet Vermouth
  3/4 oz. Sherry
  3/4 oz. Pineapple Juice

JUPITER COCKTAIL MARTINI

 1 1/2 oz. Gin
  3/4 oz. Dry Vermouth
  1 tsp. Parfait Amour or Creme
     de Violette
  1 tsp. Fresh Orange Juice

Shake ingredients with ice. Strain into chilled glass.

197

JUST PEACHY

    1 oz. Stoli Persik Vodka
splash Stoli Zinamon Vodka
Garnish with cinnamon stick.
Peggy Howell
Cotati Yacht Club & Saloon
Cotati, CA

KAHLUA DAWN MARTINI

    2 oz. Dry Gin
    1 oz. Kahlua Liqueur
    $1/2$ oz. Lemon Juice
Shake and strain. Serve with cocktail
maraschino cherry.

KANGAROO MARTINI

    $1^3/4$ oz. Vodka
    $3/4$ oz. Dry Vermouth
Twist of lemon peel.

KARAMOZOV KOFFEE MARTINI

Stoli Kafya Vodka straight up with a few
coffee beans.

KENTUCKY MARTINI

1½ oz. Maker's Mark Bourbon
½ oz. Amaretto
2 oz. Orange Slice Soda

Stir with ice; strain.

KETEL ME UP MARTINI

Ketel One Vodka
Dry Vermouth

Serve up with olive in chilled martini glass.

Hurricane Restaurant
Passagrille, FL

KETEL ONE COSMOPOLITAN MARTINI

Ketel One Vodka, chilled
Cointreau
Hint of Cranberry

Division Sixteen
Boston, MA

KETEL WHISTLE MARTINI

Ketel One Vodka
Lime
Cranberry Juice
Cointreau

Ajax Lounge
New Mexico

KEY WEST MARTINI

   3 parts Malibu Rum
   1 part Triple Sec
3 splashes Rose's Lime Juice
Serve up in a martini glass.
South Beach, FL

THE KEYWESTER MARTINI

   1 oz. Cream of Coconut
2½ oz. Bacardi Light Rum
   ¾ oz. Blue Curacao
   mist Martini & Rossi Extra Dry
         Vermouth
Garnish with a pineapple stuffed cherry
olive, foil palmtree, sand and blue water.
Keywester
Chicago, IL

KIEV COFFEE DELIGHT MARTINI

         Stoli Kafya Vodka
splashes Stoli Zinamon &
         Stoli Vanil Vodka

KING EIDER

Mix 2 parts of your very best Gin. One part King Eider Vermouth. Garnish with a twist of lemon.

Duckhorn Vineyards
St. Helena, CA

KISS IN THE DARK

> Bacardi Limón
> Martini & Rossi Extra Dry
> Vermouth
> Cherry Brandy

Stars
San Francisco, CA

KISS MARTINI

Combine $1\frac{1}{2}$ oz. Smirnoff Vodka with $\frac{1}{4}$ oz. Baileys Irish Cream. Dampen rim of Martini glass and coat with cinnamon-sugar mixture. Strain into a martini glass and serve.

KISSIN' IN THE RAIN MARTINI

$1\frac{1}{2}$ oz. Rain Vodka
$\frac{1}{2}$ oz. Marie Brizard Parfait
Amour Liqueur

Chill and serve in a martini glass with lemon twist.

THE KIWI MARTINI

Fresh kiwi fruit muddled and shaken
with Ketel One Vodka & sugar.

KNICKERBOCKER MARTINI

  1½ oz. Dry Gin
  1½ oz. French Dry Vermouth
 2 dashes Orange Bitters

Stir with ice and strain into a chilled
martini glass. Garnish with lemon peel.

The Rainbow Room
New York, NY

KNICKERBOCKER MARTINI II

  1½ oz. Smirnoff Vodka
  splash White Creme de Cacao
    dash Melon Liqueur

Chill, strain and garnish with honeydew
melon.

KREMLIN MARTINI

    2 oz. Smirnoff Vodka
  1½ oz. Creme de Cacao
  1½ oz. Half-and-Half

Shake well. Strain into chilled martini
glass.

KRIS' LIME MARTINI

  1 ¾ oz. Seagram's Lime Twisted Gin
   ¼ oz. Rose's Lime Juice
Garnish with a lime or lime twist.

K-TING

          Ketel One Vodka
          Ting (a grapefruit soda
          imported from Jamaica)
Nick and Eddie
New York, NY

KURANT EVENTS MARTINI

    1 oz. Absolut Kurant Vodka
   ½ oz. Grand Marnier
  drop of Sweet Vermouth
splash of Cranberry Juice
Shaken and strained into chilled
martini glass. Garnish with raspberry.
Michael Golondrina
Orocco Super Club
San Francisco, CA

KURANT MARTINI

1¼ oz. Absolut Kurant Vodka
    dash Extra Dry Vermouth

Pour Kurant and Vermouth over ice.
Shake or stir well. Strain and serve in a
cocktail glass. Garnish with a twist or
an olive.

L'ORANGERIE MARTINI

    Ice cold Tanqueray
    Sterling Vodka
  splash Grand Marnier
    twist Orange

Oliver's Mayflower Park Hotel
Seattle, WA

LADIES' CHOICE MARTINI

1½ oz. Absolut Vodka
    dash Martini & Rossi Extra
           Dry Vermouth
  ¼ oz. Kummel

Stir with ice and strain.

LADY GODIVA

2 oz. Smirnoff Vodka
1/2 oz. Godiva Chocolate Liqueur
1/4 oz. White Creme de Cacao
Cocoa, sprinkled
1 Hershey's Kiss, garnish

LANDING MARTINI

Beefeater Gin
splash Jose Cuervo Silver Tequila
Lemon twist
The Windsock Bar & Grill
San Diego, CA

LAST ROUND MARTINI

1 oz. Dry Gin
1 oz. Dry Vermouth
1/4 oz. Brandy
1/4 oz. Pernod

LAST TANGO MARTINI
    1½ oz. Dry Gin
      1 oz. Orange Juice
    ½ oz. Dry Vermouth
    ½ oz. Sweet Vermouth
    ½ oz. Cointreau
Shake and strain.

LAWYER LIBERATION MARTINI
    3 parts Finlandia Vodka
    1 part Midori
    3 parts Pineapple Juice
    splash Grapefruit Juice

LAZA MARTINI
    ¾ oz. Dry Gin
    ¾ oz. Dry Vermouth
    ¾ oz. Sweet Vermouth
Shake with ice. Add slice of pineapple.

LE CIEL D'AZUR
    2 oz. Skyy Vodka
    splash Blue Curacao
Brasserie Jo Martini's
Chicago, IL

LEAP YEAR MARTINI
  1¼ oz. Dry Gin
  ½ oz. Orange-flavored Gin
  ½ oz. Sweet Vermouth
  ¼ oz. Lemon Juice

LEMON AND SPICE
        Absolut Citron Vodka
        Absolut Peppar Vodka
  drop Dry Vermouth
        Lemon twist

Cecilia's
Breckenridge, CO

LEMON CHIFFON MARTINI
        Chilled Finlandia Vodka
  ¼ oz. Triple Sec
  1 oz. Sweet & Sour Mix
Squeeze and drop in fresh lemon
wedge.
Finlandia Fashion Martinis

LEMON COSMOPOLITAN MARTINI

    2 oz. Absolut Citron Vodka
    ½ oz. Cranberry Juice
    splash Triple Sec
    splash Sprite

Stir with ice and strain into a chilled martini glass. Garnish with lemon twist.
The Martini Club
Atlanta, GA

LEMON DROP MARTINI

Absolut Citron Vodka and freshly squeezed lemon with a sugar rim glass.

LEMON DROP MARTINI II

    Absolut Citron Vodka
    splash Lemonade

Serve in sugar rimmed glass with a twist.
Cecilia's
Breckenridge, CO

LEMON DROP MARTINI III

  Sugar
1 1/2 oz. Absolut Citron Vodka
  1/4 oz. Triple Sec
  1/4 oz. Sweet and Sour Mix

Wet the rim of the chilled martini glass
with water. Dip in sugar and brush off
any extra. Stir the Vodka, Triple Sec and
sweet and sour mix with ice. Strain care-
fully into the sugar-rimmed martini glass.
Tongue & Groove
Atlanta, GA

LEMON GRASS MARTINI

Freshly muddled lemon grass shaken
with Belvedere Vodka and lemon zest.
Lot 61
New York, NY

LEMONADE MARTINI

  Tanqueray Sterling Citrus
  Vodka
  Lemon Slice
  Sugar rind
Yvette Wintergarden
Chicago, IL

LEMONTINI MARTINI

    2 oz. Stoli Limonnaya Vodka
    ½ oz. Dry Vermouth
            Cointreau

Line a cocktail glass with Cointreau and pour out excess. Combine Vodka and Vermouth over ice in a mixing glass. Strain into the cocktail glass.

LENOX ROOM PEACHY KEEN MARTINI

    2 oz. Vodka
    1 tsp. Peach Puree
    3 oz. Peach Nectar

Stir with ice and strain into a chilled martini glass. Garnish with peach slice.

The Lenox Room
New York, NY

LEW'S CLASSIC MARTINI

            Beefeater Gin
            Dry Vermouth

Served chilled and up. Garnish with pimento stuffed olive.

Scott Hein, Bar Manager
LewMarNel's
South Lake Tahoe, CA

LIAR'S MARTINI
    1½ oz. Dry Gin
    ½ oz. Dry Vermouth
    ¼ oz. Orange Curacao
    ¼ oz. Sweet Vermouth
Stir gently with ice and strain.

LICIA ALBANESE MARTINI
    1½ oz. Dry Gin
    ½ oz. Campari
Twist of lemon peel. Serve over ice.

LILLET COCKTAIL MARTINI
    1½ oz. Lillet
    1 oz. Dry Gin
Twist of lemon peel.

LIME DROP
        Skyy Vodka
        Lime Juice
        Cointreau
Shake and serve with a sugared rim.
Lot 61
New York, NY

LIME LIGHT MARTINI

  6 parts Finlandia Vodka
  1 part Grapefruit Juice
  1 part Midori

Stir gently with ice and strain into
chilled glass. Garnish with thinly sliced
lemon and lime twists.

LIMÓN CRANTINI

        Bacardi Limón
        Cranberry Juice Cocktail

Martini's
New York, NY

LIMÓN MARTINI

  1½ oz. Bacardi Limón
  ½ oz. Martini & Rossi Extra Dry
          Vermouth
  splash Cranberry Juice

Shake ingredients with ice and strain
into a chilled martini glass. Garnish
with a twist of lemon peel.

"WE'VE ANALYZED DR. JECKYLL'S FORMULA...IT'S A VODKA MARTINI."

LIMONNAYA

  2¼ oz. Stoli Vodka
  ¼ oz. Sour Mix
          White Sugar

Shake with ice, serve up or on the rocks.
The Martini Club
Atlanta, GA

LIMÓN TWIST

  2 oz. Bacardi Limón
  ¼ oz. Cointreau
  ⅛ oz. Martini & Rossi Extra Dry
          Vermouth
wedge Fresh Lemon

LIMONTINI

      Stolichnaya Limonnaya
      Vodka
      Dry Vermouth
      Cointreau

LIMONTINI II

  1½ oz. Glacier Vodka
  ½ oz. Limoncello

Garnish with a lemon wedge.

LINDBERGH MARTINI

1 part Absolut Vodka
1 part Peach Schnapps
splash Orange Juice
        Orange peel

The Windsock Bar & Grill
San Diego, CA

LIQUORICE MARTINI

        Liquorice
dash Sambuca shaken with
        Belvedere Vodka

Lot 61
New York, NY

LOBOTOMY MARTINI

1 oz. Amaretto
$1/4$ oz. Chambord
$1/2$ oz. Pineapple Juice

Chill.

LOCOMOKO

    1 oz. Stoli Ohranj Vodka
    1/2 oz. Triple Sec
    1/2 oz. Lime Juice
    1 oz. Cranberry Juice
    1/2 oz. Orange Curacao
    1 oz. Orange Juice

Shake and strain over ice, blend or straight up.

Alan Hara
Club Miwa's

LONDON LEMONADE MARTINI

    2 1/2 oz. Bombay Sapphire Gin
    1 oz. Fresh Lemon Juice
    1/2 oz. Rose's Lime Juice
    1/2 oz. Cointreau

Garnish with lemon twist.

LONDON SUN MARTINI

    1 1/2 oz. Beefeater Dry Gin
    1/2 oz. Dry Sherry
    1 dash Orange Bitters

Garnish with a twist.

LONE TREE MARTINI

   1½ oz. Bombay Gin
     dash Martini & Rossi Extra Dry
          Vermouth
     dash Lemon Juice

Stir in cocktail glass. Strain & serve
straight up or on the rocks. Add lemon
twist or olives.

LONE TREE MARTINI

   2 parts Gin
    1 part Italian Vermouth
 2 dashes Lemon Juice

LOPEZ MARTINI

     ¾ Absolut Vodka
     ¼ DiSaronno Amaretto

Combine in martini glass. Serve room
or chilled temperature. Straight up.
Garnish with slice of lemon.

Pio Lopex
Mom's Ristorante
Edison, NJ

LOS ALTO MARTINI

1-2 dashes Chardonnay
1½ oz. El Tesoro Silver Tequila
1 twist Lemon
Blend & stir.

THE LOVE MARTINI

1 oz. Rain Vodka chilled
½ oz. White Creme de Cacao
¼ oz. Chambord
Serve in chilled classic martini glass.

LUCKY MOJO #99

Stoli Razberi Vodka
99 Bananas Liqueur
Chilled over ice and strained into a
martini glass.

LOUIS MARTINI

1½ oz. Dry Gin
½ oz. Dry Vermouth
¼ oz. Grand Marnier
¼ oz. Cointreau

LOUISIANA RAIN MARTINI

    2 parts Rain Vodka
    1 part Vermouth
            Generous splash of Louisiana
            Gold® Red Pepper Sauce

Shake Rain Vodka with Vermouth and
pepper sauce in martini shaker over ice.
Strain into chilled martini glass.
Garnish with red pepper (optional).
Rain Vodka
New Orleans, LA

LOYAL MARTINI

    2 oz. Ketel One Vodka
    3 drops Expensive Balsamic Vinegar

Stir gently with ice; strain.

LUCIEN GAUDIN MARTINI

    1 oz. Dry Gin
    ½ oz. Cointreau
    ½ oz. Campari
    ½ oz. Dry Vermouth

LUXURY MARTINI

Belvedere Vodka shaken and served
straight up.

LYCHEE MARTINI

Muddled lychees shaken with Belvedere Vodka & lime.

Lot 61
New York, NY

MAD 28 MARTINI

Belvedere Vodka
Passion Fruit
Hine Cognac
Cranberry Juice

MAD 28
New York, NY

MADISON MARTINI

2¼ oz. Bombay Sapphire Gin
¼ oz. Dewars Scotch

Add ice to martini glass, fill with water. In ice shaker add Scotch, shake and strain into glass and drink.

Greg Hyde
The Ripple in Stillwater
Edna, NM

MADRAS MARTINI

In glass shaker filled $\frac{1}{2}$ with ice

   $1\frac{1}{2}$ oz. Stoli Ohranj Vodka

   $1\frac{1}{2}$ oz. Finlandia Cranberry Vodka

Stir & strain into chilled martini glass.

Garnish with orange twist.

Toby Ellis
T.G.I. Friday's
Chevy Chase, MD

MAE WEST MARTINI

   2 oz. Smirnoff Vodka

   dash Melon Liqueur

   dash DiSaronno Amaretto

   dash Cranberry Juice

Chill and strain into a chilled
martini glass.

MAGIC MARTINI

   1 oz. Vodka

   $\frac{1}{2}$ oz. Kahlua

   $\frac{1}{2}$ oz. Baileys Irish Cream

   2 oz. Milk

Shaken into pre-chilled martini glass.

Pete Glavas, Bar Manager
Foghorns Bar n' Grill

MAGNIFICENT SEVEN
(WITH LEMON)

    2¼ oz. Ketel One Vodka
    splash Martini & Rossi Extra Dry
            Vermouth
    splash Sweet & Sour Mix
    splash Cranberry Juice
    splash Triple Sec
            Sugar rimmed glasses
            Fresh Lemons
            Whole Big Dash of Love

Hi Ball Lounge
San Francisco, CA

MAIDEN'S PRAYER

    1 oz. Cork Dry Gin
    ½ oz. Cointreau
    ¼ oz. Orange Juice
    ¼ oz. Lemon Juice

Shake.

MALACCA MARTINI

2½ oz. Tanqueray Malacca Gin
splash Dry Vermouth to taste
Garnish with olive or twist of lemon.

MALIBU MARTINI

Malibu Rum
Bombay Gin
Dry Vermouth
Garnish with a twist.

MALIBU RAIN MARTINI

Chilled Finlandia Vodka
1½ oz. Pineapple Juice
½ oz. Malibu
splash Orange Juice
Finlandia Fashion Martinis

MANDARIN MARTINI

1 part Godiva Liqueur
1 part Absolut Vodka
splash Cointreau or Orange Juice
Combine with ice and shake well.
Garnish with an orange slice.

MANDARIN MARTINI II

   1½ oz. Stolichnaya Cristall Vodka
    1 oz. Bombay Sapphire Gin
 1 dash Cointreau

Squeeze the juice of ¼ of a mandarin orange into the shaker (perfectionists should squeeze it through a tea strainer) Garnish with mandarin orange.

MANDERIN PENCIL SHARPENER MARTINI

          Bacardi Spice Rum
          Martini & Rossi Rosso
          Vermouth
 splash Sweet Ginger Syrup Fortify
          with gold flake and Ginseng

Garnish with a candied kumquat incased in pulled sugar.
Red Light
Chicago, IL

MANDRIN SUNSET

   1½ oz. Absolut Mandrin
   1½ oz. Watermelon Pucker
  splash OJ

Garnish with orange slice.

MANGO 'TINI

Fresh Mango
Muddled & shaken with Belvedere
Vodka & sugar.

Lot 61
New York, NY

MAPLE LEAF MARTINI

$1/2$ oz. Amaretto
$1/2$ oz. Banana Liqueur
$1/2$ oz. Cherry Liqueur
$1/2$ oz. Midori
splash Grenadine
splash Cranberry Juice
Shake ingredients.

Pete Glavas, Bar Manager
Foghorns Bar n' Grill

MARASCHINO MARTINI

Bombay Sapphire Gin splashed with
Cherry Brandy. Serve chilled and up.
Garnish with maraschino cherry.

Scott Hein, Bar Manager
LewMarNel's
South Lake Tahoe, CA

MARCINI

   1 shot Absolut Vodka
   1 shot Cuervo Tequila
             Extra, Extra Dry Vermouth
Garnish with lime.
Marcie Jackel
Woodside Inn
Trenton, NJ

MARDI GRAS SKYY MARTINI

   2 oz. Skyy Vodka
  1/8 oz. Blue Curacao
  1/2 oz. Cranberry Juice
          Fresh Lime Juice

MARGIT MARTINI

Bombay Sapphire splashed with fresh
lemon juice. Serve chilled and up with a
lemon twist.
Scott Hein, Bar Manager
LewMarNel's
South Lake Tahoe, CA

MARINERS MARTINI

Line martini glass with Grand Marnier; swirl and dump. Pour ice cold Ketel One Vodka into glass. Garnish with orange twist.

Travis Krueger
Civic Pub
Coventry, CT

MARISA'S "OUTRAGEOUS OHRANJ" MARTINI

1¾ oz.	Stolichnaya Ohranj Vodka
¼ oz.	Cointreau
2 drops	Martini & Rossi Sweet Vermouth
	Orange peel

Chill over ice, slightly shake. Strain into frozen martini glass.

Marisa Santacroce, Bar Manager
Santacroces' Italian Restaurant
Hood River, OR

MARITIME MARTINI

½ oz.	Cherry-infused Light Rum
1½ oz.	Pineapple-infused Vodka

Orange slice and maraschino cherry garnish. Blend & stir.

MARKERS MARK MARTINI
    2 oz. Markers Mark
    splash Dry Vermouth
Twist.

MARTIAN GIBSON
    Grey Goose Vodka
    splash Scotch
Garnish with an onion.
John Caine
Café Mars
San Francisco, CA

MARTINEZ COCKTAIL
    1 dash Boker's Bitters
    2 dashes Maraschino
    1 pony Old Tom Gin
    1 Wine glass of Vermouth
    2 small Lumps of Ice
Jerry Thomas' Bartenders Guide 1887 –
Could be the first martini.

"I FIND MARRIAGE AND MARTINIS
ARE A VERY GOOD MIX."

MARTINI CARIB

  1¼ oz. Cane Juice Vodka
  ¾ oz. Key Largo Schnapps
Garnish with 3 grapes.
Stephen Dale
Bahama Breeze
Winter Park, FL

MARTINI "MANOU"

    Stoli Razberi Vodka
    Massenez Framboise

MARTINI AU CHOCOLATE

    Godiva Liqueur
    Stoli Vanil Vodka
Garnish with a dusting of Cocoa.
Brasserie Jo Martini's
Chicago, IL

MARTINI DE MURE

    Absolut Kurant
Lace with Creme de Mure
(blackberry liqueur).
Brasserie Jo Martini's
Chicago, IL

MARTINI JO

Stolichnaya Vodka

A whisper of Lillet Rouge and an
orange twist.

Brasserie Jo Martini's
Chicago, IL

MARTINI MELON

Finlandia Vodka

With a soupcon of Midori and OJ.

Brasserie Jo Martini's
Chicago, IL

MARTINI MINT

2 oz. Gin or Vodka

1 oz. Peppermint Schnapps

Combine both ingredients in a mixing
glass with ice cubes. Stir and strain into
a chilled cocktail glass.

MARTINI PERNOD

Beefeater Gin

dash Pastis

(The cocktail of Provence.)

Brasserie Jo Martini's
Chicago, IL

MARTINI PICANTE

>   Absolut Peppar Vodka

Serve with jalapeño & olive.

Sheraton Seattle
Seattle, WA

MARTINI REFRESHER

   1½ oz. Gin
    ½ oz. Dry Vermouth
    ½ oz. Sweet Vermouth
   1 drop Peppermint Extract

Combine Vermouth, Gin and peppermint over ice cubes in mixing glass.
Strain into martini glass. Garnish with
1 or 2 mint leaves.

Judy Bernas
Tucson, AZ

MARTINI WITH A KICK

>   Absolut Peppar Vodka
   hint Dry Vermouth

Garnish with hot, red chili pepper
stuffed olives.

Shulas No Name Lounge
Tampa, FL

MAUI MARTINI

    2 oz. Smirnoff Vodka
splash Blue Curacao
splash Grand Marnier
splash Grapefruit Juice
Garnish with a twist of lime.

MAURICE MARTINI

  2 parts Dry Gin
   1 part French Vermouth
   1 part Italian Vermouth
          Juice of $\frac{1}{4}$ Orange

MAXIM MARTINI

  2 parts Dry Gin
   1 part Italian Vermouth
2 dashes White Creme de Cacao

McKEEGANS DREAM

  $1\frac{1}{2}$ oz. Bombay Sapphire
          (or Absolut)
  $\frac{1}{4}$ oz. Bushmills
Shake and strain into martini glass.
Brett Egan, Director
National Bartenders School
Lakewood, CA

MELLOW YELLOW MARTINI

    2 oz. Gilbey's Gin
    1 oz. Kina Lillet Blanc
    1 drop Angostura Bitters
Stir gently, don't shake. Serve in martini glass.

MELON MARTINI

            Finlandia Vodka
            Midori
Garnish with a lemon twist.
Bally's
Las Vegas, NV

MELOTINI

    ½ oz. Midori Melon Liqueur
    1 oz. Martini & Rossi Extra Dry
            Vermouth
    ½ oz. Pineapple Juice
    ⅓ oz. Lemon Juice
    dash Angostura Bitters
Mix in stirring glass. Strain into an iced cocktail glass. Add a Zest of lemon and spring mint.
Bogdan Dadynski
Trier, Germany

MENTHE

    1 oz. Dry Gin
    1 oz. Dry Vermouth
    ¼ oz. White Creme de Menthe
Sprig of mint garnish.

MERMAID

    1 oz. Stoli Ohranj Vodka
    ¼ oz. Blue Curacao
    2 oz. Pineapple Juice
Shaken in silver shaker. Garnish with
pineapple chunk.
Maureen & Stephen Horn
Mermaid Martini Bar, Spiaggi,
Cape May, NJ

MERRY MARTINI

    ½ to 1 oz. Dry Vermouth
    2 oz. Burnett's London Dry Gin
Shake well with ice, and strain into
martini glass. Add olive or fresh
cranberry.

MERVYN-TINI

Stolichnaya Pertsovka Vodka
Dry Vermouth
Caper berry

No. 18
New York, NY

METROPOLIS MARTINI

1½ oz. Vodka
½ oz. Strawberry Liqueur
Chill, strain and top with 1 oz.
Champagne; garnish with a strawberry.

METROPOLIS

Creme de Framboise
Raspberry eau de vie
Stoli Razberi Vodka topped with
Champagne.
Lot 61
New York, NY

METROPOLITAN

2 oz. OP.
¼ oz. Brandy
¼ oz. Sweet Vermouth
½ tsp. Simple Syrup
Shake with ice. Strain or serve on the
rocks.

METROPOLITAN MARTINI

Skyy Vodka

Strawberry Liqueur

Float Champagne

Served up in an oversized chilled stem.
Shaken, not stirred.

Skyy Martini List

MEXICAN ICE CUBE

1 oz. Stoli Kafya Vodka

1 oz. Kahlua

4 scoops Coffee ice cream

1 can Mandarin Oranges (strained)

4 oz. Orange Juice

Mix ingredients in blender until
creamy. Pour into shaker glass.
Garnish with a slice.

Reid Jutras
Octane Inter Lounge
Rockford, IL

MEXICAN MARTINI

A dash of Jose Cuervo Gold Tequila
poured into a chilled Martini glass. Top
with 2 oz. Smirnoff Vodka. Garnish
with a Jalapeño Pepper.

MEXICO MARTINI

    1½ oz. Gran Centenario
              Plata Tequila
    1 tbsp. Extra Dry Vermouth
2-3 drops Vanilla Extract

Shake and strain into an iced glass.

MIAMI BEACH MARTINI

   ¾ oz. Scotch
   ¾ oz. Dry Vermouth
   ¾ oz. Unsweetened Grapefruit Juice

Shake ingredients with ice. Strain into chilled glass.

MIAMI BLUE MOON

         Skyy Vodka
         Blue Curacao
   dash Grand Marnier

Hamiltons
Miami, FL

MICHELANGELO MARTINI

    1½ oz. Smirnoff Vodka
   splash Campari
    ⅓ oz. Orange Juice

Combine, strain and serve with orange wedge.

MICKEY FINN MARTINI
  1½ oz. Absolut Vodka
    dash Martini & Rossi Extra Dry
          Vermouth
  splash Hiram Walker White Creme
          de Menthe

Stir with ice and strain. Garnish with mint.

MIDNIGHT MARTINI
  ¾ oz. Dry Gin
  ¾ oz. Sweet Vermouth
  ¾ oz. Dry Vermouth
  ¼ oz. Pernod
  1 dash Orange Juice

MIDNIGHT MARTINI II
  1½ oz. Smirnoff Vodka
    dash Coffee Liqueur
  splash Orange Liqueur

Chill, strain and garnish with an orange wheel.

MIDNIGHT MARTINI III

   $1\frac{1}{2}$ oz. Vodka
   $\frac{1}{2}$ oz. Chambord

Stir with ice and strain. Garnish with lemon twist.

Gallery Lounge Sheraton
Seattle, WA

MIDNITE MARTINI

   $1\frac{1}{4}$ oz. Glacier Vodka
   $\frac{3}{4}$ oz. Echte Kroatzbeer Blackberry
            Liqueur

Stir ingredients with ice. Strain into a chilled cocktail glass.

MIDNIGHT SUN MARTINI

   5 parts Finlandia Cranberry Vodka
   1 part Classic Finlandia Vodka
   1 part Kahlua

Stir with ice and strain.

MILANO MARTINI

Pour a dash of Campari and Cinzano into a chilled glass of Gin.

MILE HIGH MARTINI

1 part Stoli Vodka
1 part Absolut Vodka
1 part Skyy Vodka

Shaken and stirred. Topped with an olive.

The Windsock Bar & Grill
San Diego, CA

MILKY WAY MARTINI

Ketel One Vodka
dash Godiva and Baileys Irish Cream

Garnish with chocolate chips.

John Dourney
The Thirsty Turtle
Bernardsville, NJ

MILLION DOLLAR BABY MARTINI

1½ oz. Gin
¾ oz. Sweet Vermouth
¾ oz. Unsweetened Pineapple Juice
1 tsp. Grenadine
1 Egg White

Vigorously shake ingredients with cracked ice. Strain into chilled glass.

MINITINI

2 parts Bombay Gin
1 part White Creme de Menthe

The Windsock Bar & Grill
San Diego, CA

MINT CHOCOLATE KISS MARTINI

2 oz. Grey Goose Vodka
1 oz. White Creme de Cacao
1/4 oz. Green Creme de Menthe

Shake over ice and strain. Serve with a chocolate stick.

Pete Savoie and Adryann Omar
Top of the Hub
Boston, MA

MINT MARTINI

1 part Godiva Liqueur
1 part Absolut Vodka
splash White Creme de Menthe

Combine with ice and shake well. Serve straight up. Garnish with a mint leaf.

MINTINI

   1¾ oz. Vodka
   splash Grand Marnier
   splash White Creme de Menthe
Chill and serve up in martini glass.
Garnish with maraschino cherry.
Mike Henry
Planet Hollywood
Atlantic City, NJ

MISTICO MARTINI

   1 oz. Jose Cuervo Mistico
   1 oz. Chambord
   1 oz. Sweet & Sour Mix
Stir with ice and strain into a martini
glass.

MISTLETOE MARTINI

   4 oz. Rain Vodka
   ½ oz. Midori
   dash Grenadine
Mix Vodka and Midori over ice. Stir
and strain. Add drop of Grenadine
which will descend to the bottom
of glass.
Rain Vodka
New Orleans, LA

MOCHA 'TINI'
Freshly ground coffee beans shaken
with Skyy Vodka and Creme de Cacao.
Lot 61
New York, NY

MO COCKTAIL
	Ketel One Vodka
splash	Chambord
5 squeezes	Lemon Juice

Chill until very cold. Serve straight up
with a twist.
Mo McLaughlin
Anchovies

MOCHATINI
1½ oz.	Bacardi Light Rum
1½ oz.	Bacardi Spice Rum
1 oz.	Obilio Caffee
dash	Martini & Rossi Extra Dry Vermouth

Shaw's Crab House
Chicago, IL

MODDER COCKTAIL MARTINI

1½ oz. Dry Gin
½ oz. Dry Vermouth
½ oz. Dubonnet

Twist of lemon peel.

MOJITO MARTINI

Juice of ½ Lime
1 tsp. Sugar
2 oz. White Rum
Soda Water

Place lime juice and sugar in tall glass and stir until sugar is dissolved. Rub mint leaves around inside of glass and discard. Fill glass with crushed ice, add Rum and stir. Top with soda water. Garnish with sprig of mint.

MONEALIZÉ

½ oz. Alizé
½ oz. Southern Comfort
1 oz. Pineapple Juice
1 oz. Orange Juice

Martini glass, shaken, not stirred. Garnish with orange and maraschino cherry.

MONEYPENNEY

   1¼ oz. Smirnoff Vodka
  splash Raspberry Liqueur
    dash Cranberry Juice
Chill, strain and garnish with a
maraschino cherry.

MONKEY BAR'S BANANA MARTINI

  2½ oz. Skyy Vodka
   ½ oz. Creme de Banana
   ½ oz. Martini & Rossi Extra Dry
           Vermouth
           Caramelized Banana

Reebok Sports Clubs

MONKEY BUSINESS MARTINI

           Chilled Finlandia Arctic
           Cranberry Vodka
   ¼ oz. Malibu
   1 oz. Pineapple Juice

Finlandia Vodka Americas, Inc.
New York, NY

MONKEY SHINE MARTINI

    3 parts Classic Finlandia Vodka
    splash   Peppermint Schnapps
    3 parts Seltzer
Finlandia Martini Recipes

MONTEGO BAY MARTINI

            Malibu Rum
            Triple Sec
            Fresh Lime Juice
            Bar Sugar – Colored Sugar
            Rimmed Glass

MONTGOMERY MARTINI

    3 oz.   Gordon's Gin
    1 tsp. plus a few drops Noilly Prat
            Vermouth
    1   Olive

MONTGOMERY MARTINI II

            Tanqueray Gin chilled until
            ice cold
            Glance of Vermouth
Garnish with olive, twist or onion.
Renaissance Atlanta Hotel
Atlanta, GA

MONTMARTRE COCKTAIL MARTINI

   1½ oz. Gin
    ½ oz. Sweet Vermouth
    ½ oz. Triple Sec
           Maraschino Cherry

Shake liquid ingredients with ice. Strain into chilled glass. Garnish with maraschino cherry.

MONTPELIER MARTINI

   1¼ oz. Dry Gin
    ¾ oz. Dry Vermouth
           Cocktail Onion

MOONSHINE MARTINI

   1¾ oz. Dry Gin
    ½ oz. Dry Vermouth
    ¼ oz. Maraschino Cherry Juice
 2 dashes Pernod

MORGAN'S MARTINI

   1½ oz. Vodka
    ½ oz. Midori
   touch Dry Vermouth

Larry Clark
Morgans Tavern
Middletown, VA

MORNING COCKTAIL

    1 oz. Brandy
    1 oz. Dry Vermouth
   1/4 tsp. Pernod or other anise-
           flavored liqueur
   1/4 tsp. Maraschino Cherry Juice
   1/4 tsp. Triple Sec
2 dashes Orange Bitters
           Maraschino Cherry

Stir or shake liquid ingredients with ice.
Strain into chilled glass over ice cubes.
Garnish with maraschino cherry.

MORNING GLORY MARTINI

  1 1/2 oz. Gin
    1 oz. Stoli Vanil Vodka
   1/2 oz. Calvados

Garnish with cinnamon stick.

Chris Golz
Forbidden Fruit
Long Beach, CA

MOSQUITO MARTINI

   1½ oz. Vodka
   ⅛ oz. Cointreau
  2 drops Tabasco Pepper Sauce
  squeeze Lime Wedge

Stir and strain into chilled martini glass.
Garnish with a sliced jalapeño.

MOTHER'S DAY MARTINI

   3 oz. Grey Goose Vodka
  1 dash Dry Vermouth
  1 dash Rose Water
  3 fresh Rose Petals

Combine ingredients in a mixing glass.
Stir gently. Strain into a chilled martini
glass. Garnish with rose petals.
Albert Trummer
Danube Restaurant & Bar
New York, NY

MOULIN ROUGE MARTINI

  1½ oz. Sloe Gin
  ¾ oz. Sweet Vermouth
 3 dashes Angostura Bitters

Stir, strain into chilled glass.

MOUSSELLINI MARTINI
Bombay Sapphire Gin splashed with
Tuaca. Serve chilled and up with
a twist of lime.
Scott Hein, Bar Manager
LewMarNel's
South Lake Tahoe, CA

MRS. ROBINSON MARTINI
  1½ oz. Smirnoff Vodka
  splash Orange Juice
  splash Galliano
Chill, strain and garnish with an
orange wedge.

MUD PUDDLE MARTINI
  1 part Rain Vodka chilled
  1 part Frangelico chilled
Strain into a martini glass. Add
dash of Kahlua.

MUDDY WATERS
>   Ketel One Vodka
>   Black Sambuca

Yvette Wintergarden
Chicago, IL

MUSKOVY MARTINI
>   1 oz. Stoli Zinamon Vodka
>   1 oz. Stoli Ohranj Vodka
> $\frac{1}{2}$ oz. Triple Sec
> $\frac{1}{2}$ oz. Orange Juice

Garnish with a pinch of cinnamon &
orange twist.

MUSCOVY NEAPOLITAN
Equal parts of Stoli Razberi Vodka,
Vanil and Kafya Vodka.

MY PERSONAL MARTINI
>   2 oz. Fris Vodka
> $\frac{1}{2}$ oz. Glen Devron 15 year Single
>   Malt Scotch

Served up, very chilled, with a lemon
twist.

Kasen Price
E-mail

MY SECRET GODDESS OF LOVE

2 oz.	Stoli Razberi Vodka
1/2 oz.	Stoli Persik Vodka
3 dashes	Grenadine
1 splash	Cranberry Juice
1 splash	Pineapple Juice
1 dash	Orange Juice

Iris Vourlatos
E-mail

MYRNA LOY MARTINI

2 oz.	Smirnoff Vodka
splash	Lillet

Chill, strain and garnish with an orange peel.

MYSTIQUE MARTINI

2 oz.	Smirnoff Vodka
dash	Chartreuse

Chill, strain and garnish with a lemon or lime twist.

MYSTIRIUOS JESSY

   1 oz. Stoli Vodka
   ½ oz. Baileys Irish Cream
   ¼ oz. Frangelico
   ¼ oz. Dark Creme de Cacao

Shake ingredients on ice and serve straight up in martini glass. Garnish with cherries.

Alex Refojo
Club Mystique
Miami, FL

NAKED GLACIER MARTINI

  7 parts Classic Finlandia Vodka
   splash Peppermint Schnapps

Frost martini glass rim with superfine sugar.

NAPOLEON MARTINI

   ½ oz. Dubonnet Rouge
   ½ oz. Grand Marnier
  1½ oz. Gin
  1 twist Lemon

Blend & stir.

NAUGHTY MARTINI

    1¼ oz. Stoli Razberi Vodka
     ¾ oz. Midori
            Cranberry Juice
  splash Sour Mix

Float lemon wheel.

Evan Horton
Pleasure Island Jazz Co.
Kissimmee, FL

NAVAL COCKTAIL MARTINI

    1½ oz. Smirnoff Vodka Black
     dash Martini & Rossi Rosso
            Vermouth

Stir in cocktail glass. Strain and serve
straight up or on the rocks. Add onion
or lemon twist.

NEGRONI MARTINI

  2 parts Martini & Rossi Sweet
            Vermouth
  2 parts Gin or Vodka
   1 part Campari

Pour over ice, stir well, and strain;
garnish with a twist.

NEMO WHITE CHOCOLATE MARTINI

    5 oz. Grey Goose Vodka
    2 oz. Godiva White Chocolate
           Liqueur

Pour both ingredients over ice into mixer. Shake 3-4 times, swirl and pour. Rim glass with white chocolate.

Adrian Mishek
Nemo
Miami, FL

NEON MARTINI

    2 oz. Stoli Ohranj Vodka
    ½ oz. Blue Curacao
    ½ oz. White Creme de Cacao

Garnish with orange twist.

NEW YORKER MARTINI

    1½ oz. Dry Vermouth
    ½ oz. Dry Gin
    ½ oz. Dry Sherry
    1 dash Cointreau

Shake with ice and strain. Garnish with parsley.

NEWBURY MARTINI

    1 oz. Gin
    1 oz. Sweet Vermouth
  1/4 tsp. Cointreau
          Orange Slice

Shake liquid ingredients with cracked
ice. Strain into chilled glass. Garnish
with orange slice.

NIGHT SHIFT MARTINI

  2 1/2 oz. Bombay Sapphire Gin
    splash Galliano

Stir with ice and strain into a chilled
martini glass. Garnish with olive.
Club 36
San Francisco, CA

NIGHTMARE MARTINI

  1 1/2 oz. Gin
   1/2 oz. Madeira
   1/2 oz. Cherry Brandy
    2 tsp. Fresh Orange Juice

Shake ingredients with ice. Strain into
chilled glass.

NINETEENTH HOLE MARTINI

1½ oz. Dry Gin
½ oz. Dry Vermouth
½ oz. Sweet Vermouth
dash Angostura

Stir, strain and serve with black olive and flag.

NINOTCHKA MARTINI

1½ oz. Smirnoff Vodka
½ oz. White Creme de Cacao
splash Lemon Juice

Chill and strain into martini glass.

NO. 18 MARTINI

Absolut Citron Vodka
Grand Marnier
Orange Slice

No. 18, New York, NY

NO. 5

1 oz. Ketel One Vodka
½ oz. Bacardi Limón
½ oz. Amaretto
½ oz. Tuaca
2 drops Martini and Rossi Dry Vermouth

Garnish with rose petal.

Ralph Vega
Palace Nite Club, El Paso, TX

NOME MARTINI

   7 parts Dry Gin
   1 part Dry Sherry
   1 dash Chartreuse

Shake with ice. Serve straight up or on the rocks.

NUMBER 3 MARTINI

   1¾ oz. Dry Gin
   ½ oz. Dry Vermouth
   ¼ oz. Anisette
   1 dash Angostura Bitters

NUMBER 6 MARTINI

   1¾ oz. Dry Gin
   ½ oz. Sweet Vermouth
   ¼ oz. Orange Curacao
   twist Lemon Peel
         Orange Peel
         Maraschino Cherry

NUPTIAL BLISS MARTINI

   1½ oz. Dry Vermouth
   ½ oz. Kirsch
   1 oz. Each of Cointreau,
         Orange Juice, Lemon Juice

Shake and strain.

NUT HOUSE MARTINI

      Chilled Finlandia Arctic
      Cranberry Vodka
1/4 oz. Amaretto

Finlandia Vodka Americas, Inc.
New York, NY

NUTTINI MARTINI

2 oz. Smirnoff Vodka
1/4 oz. DiSaronno Amaretto

Chill, strain and garnish with an orange
wedge.

NUTTINI MARTINI II

      Stolichnaya Vodka
splash Frangelico
      Orange twist

Cecilia's
Breckenridge, CO

NUTTY BACARDI SPICE MARTINI

2 1/2 oz. Bacardi Spice Rum
1/2 oz. Hazelnut Liqueur

Shake and strain over ice. Serve
straight up.

NUTTY MARTINI

    1 part Godiva Liqueur
    1 part Absolut Vodka
    splash Frangelico or Amaretto
Combine with ice; shake well. Serve
chilled; garnish with three almonds.

OAHU HURRICANE MARTINI

    4 parts Gordon's Gin
    1 part French Vermouth
    1 part Italian Vermouth
    1 tsp. Pineapple Juice
Stir.

OHRANJ MARTINI

    1½ oz. Stolichnaya Ohranj Vodka
    dash Extra Dry Vermouth
    splash Triple Sec
        Orange peel
Shake with ice and strain; serve up or
on the rocks.

OLD ESTONIAN MARTINI

   1$\frac{1}{4}$ oz. Dry Gin
   1$\frac{1}{4}$ oz. Lillet
 2 dashes Orange Bitters
 2 dashes Creme de Noyaux
          Orange peel

OLD-FASHIONED MARTINI

    2 oz. Smirnoff Vodka
          Equal splash of Sweet
          Vermouth and Dry Vermouth
Strain and garnish with a lemon twist.

OLIVER TWIST MARTINI

Dribble Dry Vermouth over ice in rocks
glass. Strain. Add Beefeater Gin to top.
No garnish.
Mr. G's Lounge
Deltona, FL

OLIVER'S CLASSIC MARTINI

   2½ oz. Bombay Sapphire Gin or
              Stolichnaya Cristall Vodka
   ¼ oz. Cinzano Dry Vermouth
  2 large Vermouth marinated Italian
              olives

Pour Vermouth into empty martini mixing glass. Swirl to coat inside of glass and dispose of excess. Fill coated glass with ice. Pour Gin or Vodka over ice, shake vigorously and let stand 20 seconds. Garnish with olives and strain mixture into glass over olives.

Oliver's
Mayflower Park Hotel
Seattle, WA

OLIVER'S TWIST

           Absolut Citron Vodka
           Perfect twist of fresh lemon

Oliver's
Mayflower Park Hotel
Seattle, WA

OLYMPIC MARTINI

  1¾ oz. Dry Gin
   ½ oz. Sweet Vermouth
   ¼ oz. Pernod

OLYMPIC GOLD

1 oz. Bombay Sapphire Gin
1½ oz. Absolut Citron Vodka
⅓ oz. Canton Ginger Liqueur
⅙ oz. Martell Cordon Bleu Cognac
1 Lemon twist

Michael Vezzoni
The Four Seasons Olympic Hotel
Seattle, WA

ON THE RUNWAY

Stoli Ohranj Vodka
splash Campari
splash OJ

Lemon twist garnish.
The Windsock Bar & Grill
San Diego, CA

ON TIME MARTINI

Bombay Sapphire Gin
1 part Vermouth
Olive

The Windsock Bar & Grill
San Diego, CA

ONE EXCITING NIGHT MARTINI

    3/4 oz. Dry Gin
    3/4 oz. Dry Vermouth
    3/4 oz. Sweet Vermouth
    1/4 oz. Orange Juice
    twist Lemon peel

Coat the rim of the glass with sugar before mixing.

ONE MARTINI, STRAIGHT UP WITH A TWIST

Chill a martini glass with ice and Vermouth. Shake Ketel One in a shaker with ice until frost forms on the outside. Dump ice and Vermouth from the glass. Strain in Vodka. Garnish with a twist.

OPAL

    2 oz. OP.
    1/2 oz. White Creme de Menthe

Shake with ice. Serve straight-up or on the rocks.

OPERA MARTINI

   1½ oz. Gin
   ½ oz. Dubonnet Rouge
   1 tsp. Maraschino Cherry Juice

Stir or shake with ice. Strain into chilled glass.

ORANGEBERRY 'TINI

Fresh strawberries & orange shaken with Belvedere Vodka.

Lot 61
New York, NY

ORANGE BOAR

   2 oz. Gordon's Orange
           Flavored Gin
   ¼ oz. Martini & Rossi Sweet
           Vermouth
  splash Stoli Vanil Vodka

Matt Hoy
Sweetwaters Restaurant
Eau Claire, WI

ORANGE BOWL

                Tanqueray Gin or Gordon's
                Orange Vodka
                Vermouth
    splash Grand Marnier
Garnish with orange slice.
Shulas No Name Lounge
Tampa, FL

ORANGE DELIGHT

                Stoli Ohranj Vodka
    splash Dark Creme de Cacao
Garnish with fresh orange wedge.
Squirrel Morgan
Pier St. Pub
West Palm Beach, FL

ORANGE DELITE

    1 oz. Stoli Ohranj Vodka
    ¾ oz. Triple Sec
    ½ oz. Amaretto
    2 oz. Orange Juice
Combine ingredients over ice. Top with
splash of soda water.
Lee Tepfer
E-mail

ORANGE MARTINI KICK

    2 oz. Stoli Ohranj Vodka in glass
            shaker with ice
    1/2 oz. Sambuca

Shake and strain into chilled martini
glass. Rub rind of orange on rim of glass.
Mike Polhamus
Bennigans
Fairfield, NJ

ORANGE MARTINI

    1 1/2 oz. Gordon's Orange Vodka
    1/4 oz. Triple Sec
    1/4 oz. Martini & Rossi Sweet
            Vermouth

Shake with ice and strain into martini
glass. Garnish with orange twist.
Sam King
Bellingham, WA

ORANGE MARTINI II

    1 1/2 oz. Gordon's Orange Vodka
    dash Extra Dry Vermouth
    splash Triple Sec
        Orange peel

Shake with ice and strain. Serve up
or on the rocks.

ORANGE MARTINI III

   2 oz. Vodka
   1 tsp. Grand Marnier
           Orange Peel
           Cracked Ice

Chill martini glass. Mix Vodka and Grand Marnier with ice. Shake vigorously. Take chilled martini glass and rub inside with orange peel. Shake again and strain into martini glass. Garnish with 3 dried cherries.

Todd Greeno
New York, NY

ORANGE MOCHATINI

   2 oz. Stoli Kafya Vodka
   1 oz. Stoli Vanil Vodka
 1 splash Chocolate Liqueur
 1 splash Orange Liqueur

Garnish with 3 coffee beans or orange twist.

ORANGE TRUFFLE

> Mixture of Orange-flavored
> Vodka
> White-Chocolate Liqueur

The Velvet Lounge
Detroit, MI

ORANGETINI

1½ oz. Absolut Vodka
dash Martini & Rossi Extra Dry
Vermouth
splash Hiram Walker Triple Sec

Stir gently and strain over ice. Garnish
with an orange peel.

OHRANJ YOU SPECIAL

1 oz. Stoli Ohranj Vodka
splash Grand Marnier

Garnish with shaved orange peel.
Peggy Howell
Cotati Yacht Club & Saloon
Cotati, CA

ORCHID PETAL

    1½ oz. OP.
    ½ oz. Raspberry Liqueur or
              Chambord

Shake with ice. Serve straight up or on the rocks.

ORIGINAL MARTINEZ COCKTAIL

1 part	Old Tom Gin
1 part	Sweet Vermouth
2 dashes	Simple Syrup
1 dash	Maraschino Juice
1 dash	Angostura Bitters
1 slice	Lemon

ORIGINAL SIN MARTINI

Equal parts Apple Barrel Schnapps and Vodka.

OYSTER MARTINI

Frosty Skyy Vodka martini. Shaken and poured over freshly shucked oyster from the raw bar.

Eastside West
San Francisco, CA

OZZON MARTINI

  2¹⁄₂ oz. Skyy Vodka
  splash Romana Sambuca
      1 Olive for garnish

Stir with ice and strain into a chilled martini glass. Garnish with olive.

Club 36
San Francisco, CA

PAISLEY

  2 oz. Bombay Sapphire Gin
  ¹⁄₂ oz. Single Malt Scotch Whisky
  ¹⁄₂ oz. Dry Vermouth

Garnish with a twist.

PALL MALL MARTINI

1½ oz. Gin
½ oz. Dry Vermouth
½ oz. Sweet Vermouth
1 tsp. White Creme de Menthe
1 dash Angostura Bitters, optional

Stir ingredients with ice.

PALMETTO MARTINI

1½ oz. Rum
1 oz. Sweet Vermouth
2 dashes Bitters

Chill, strain and serve in a chilled glass;
garnish with a lemon twist.

PANACHE MARTINI

2½ oz. Grey Goose Vodka
¼ oz. Pernod
¼ oz. White Creme de Menthe
whisper Dry Vermouth

*Gary Marcarelli of the Meridien Hotel,
Boston, MA*

PARADIGM SHIFT

"Entering an alternative Martini dimension."

1/8 oz.	Campari
1 oz.	Fresh Squeezed Texas Ruby Red Grapefruit Juice
1 oz.	Fresh in-house made Raspberry Lemon-Lime Sour
2 oz.	Rain Vodka
3/4 oz.	Bombay Gin

Start with an empty ice cold Martini mixing glass. Lightly coat the mixing glass with Campari. Swirl to coat inside of mixing glass with Campari; dispose of excess. Fill mixing glass with ice. Squeeze Texas Ruby Red Grapefruit into glass. Add fresh raspberry lemon-lime sour. Pour Rain Vodka & Bombay Gin into mixing glass. Cap and shake vigorously. Strain the mixture into frozen martini glass. Garnish with frozen grapefruit slice and fresh frozen raspberry.

Oliver's
Mayflower Park Hotel
Seattle, WA

277

PARIS CARVER MARTINI

    2 oz. Smirnoff Vodka

  splash Romana Black Sambuca

Run a lime wedge around the rim of a
martini glass and coat with sugar. Chill,
strain and garnish with a lime.

PARISIAN KISS MARTINI

    2 oz. Smirnoff Vodka

  splash Pernod

Chill, strain and sprinkle with juniper
berries.

PARISIAN MARTINI

    1 oz. Gin

    1 oz. Dry Vermouth

    1 oz. Creme de Cassis

Chill and strain into a chilled
martini glass.

PARISIAN MARTINI II

  $2\frac{1}{2}$ oz. Tanqueray Gin

    dash Pernod

      1 Tomolive for garnish

Stir with ice and strain into a chilled
martini glass. Garnish with Tomolive.

Compass Rose
San Francisco, CA

PARK AVENUE MARTINI

    1½ oz. Gin
    ½ oz. Sweet Vermouth
    1 oz. Pineapple Juice
2 -3 drops Curacao
Chill and strain into a chilled martini glass.

PARK PLACE MARTINI

    1 oz. Bombay Sapphire Gin
    1 oz. Chambord
    dash Triple Sec
    1 Lemon Zest

PASHA MARTINI

    2 oz. Grey Goose Vodka
    1 oz. Midori
Shake rapidly over ice. Pour in ½-1 oz.
Chambord. No garnish.
Jim Bacus of Pasha
Chicago, IL

PARROT HEAD

        Midori
        Malibu
        Pineapple Juice
        Grenadine
Gatsby
Boca Raton, FL

PASSION FRUIT MARTINI
Vodka, Alizé with just a hint of Remy
Martin and cranberry juice.

PATSY'S MARTINI
  1½ oz. Stoli Vodka
    1 oz. Champagne
The Martini Club
Atlanta, GA

PEACH DREAM MARTINI
    1 oz. Stoli Persik Vodka
  splash Peach Schnapps
  splash Malibu Rum
Serve on the rocks strained in a chilled
"up" glass.
Eric Schmidt
Café Winberie
Oak Park, IL

PEACHES & CREAM
  1½ oz. Stoli Persik Vodka
   ½ oz. Stoli Vanil Vodka
     1 peach slice as garnish
Club XIX at the Lodge at Pebble Beach
Pebble Beach, CA

PEACH FUZZ

       Stoli Persik Vodka
       Peach Schnapps
       Triple Sec
splash Orange Juice

Gatsby
Boca Raton, FL

PEACH HIGHRISE MARTINI

2 oz. Stoli Persik Vodka
splash Cranberry Juice
splash Fresh Lime Juice
       Lime Wedge

PEACH MARTINI

       Skyy Vodka
       Peach Schnapps

Portland's Best
Portland, OR

PEACHIE-KEEN MARTINI

       Chilled Finlandia Artic
       Cranberry Vodka
1/4 oz. Peach Schnapps

Finlandia Vodka Americas, Inc.
New York, NY

PEAR MARTINI

    2 oz. Grey Goose Vodka
    ½ oz. Cointreau
    ½ oz. Fresh Squeezed Lime Juice
Rim glass with sugar and dried orange rind.
Thomas Mastricola of 9 Park
Boston, MA

PEAR MARTINI II

    2 oz. Stolichnaya Vodka
    ½ oz. Perle de Brillet Liqueur
Garnish with pear slice.

PEAR MARTINI III

    Ketel One Vodka
    Flavor with dash of Perle de
    Brillet, (a pear/Cognac liqueur)
    Lemon twist
Renaissance Atlanta Hotel
Atlanta, GA

PEATINI

    1 oz. Gin
    splash Vermouth
Shake with crushed ice, pour into glass.
1 Texas sized black-eye pea.
Marianne Stevens
E-mail

PEGGY MARTINI

   $1\frac{1}{2}$ oz. Dry Gin
   $\frac{3}{4}$ oz. Dry Vermouth
   $\frac{1}{4}$ oz. Pernod
   $\frac{1}{4}$ oz. Dubonnet

PEPPAR MARTINI

   Absolut Peppar Vodka
   Dry Vermouth
Garnish with Jalapeño Stuffed Olive.

PEPPERMINT MARTINI

   2 oz. Vodka
   $\frac{1}{2}$ oz. Rumple Minze
Shake.

PEPPERMINT PATTY MARTINI

   $2\frac{1}{2}$ oz. Grey Goose Vodka
   $\frac{1}{2}$ oz. Peppermint Schnapps
   $\frac{1}{2}$ oz. White Creme de Cacao
Garnish with two Junior Mints on a
pick.
Michael Mika
Harvey's
Boston, MA

PEPPERTINI

$1\frac{1}{2}$ oz. Stoli Pertsovka Vodka
$\frac{1}{2}$ oz. Dry Vermouth
Olive garnish

Mix Pertsovka and Dry Vermouth in
cocktail shaker over ice, stir and strain.

PERFECT MARTINI

$1\frac{3}{4}$ oz. Gin
$\frac{1}{4}$ oz. Sweet Vermouth
$\frac{1}{4}$ oz. Dry Vermouth
1 twist Lemon

Blend & stir.

PERFECT MARTINI II

2 oz. Dry Gin
$\frac{1}{4}$ oz. French Vermouth
$\frac{1}{4}$ oz. Italian Vermouth
1 dash Bitters

Twist of lemon peel.

PERFECT MARTINI III

    4 oz. Bombay Sapphire Gin
    1 oz. each: French and Italian
            Vermouth
1 dash Orange Bitters
Garnish with orange twist.

PERFECT PAIR

1½ oz. Grey Goose Vodka
 ½ oz. Pear Eau de Vie
 ½ oz. Fresh Lemon Juice
 ½ oz. Simple Syrup
splash Orange Juice

Marco Dianysos
Absinthe
San Francisco, CA

PERFECT ROYAL MARTINI

¾ oz. Dry Gin
¾ oz. Dry Vermouth
¾ oz. Sweet Vermouth
¼ oz. Pernod
       Green Cherry

PERFECTION MARTINI

$1\frac{1}{2}$ oz. Bombay Gin
dash Martini & Rossi Rosso
        Vermouth

Stir in cocktail glass. Strain & serve straight up or on the rocks. Add lemon twist or olives.

PERFECTION MARTINI II

$1\frac{3}{4}$ oz. Dry Gin
$\frac{1}{2}$ oz. Sweet Vermouth
$\frac{1}{2}$ oz. Orange Juice

PERNOD MARTINI

2 oz. Dry Gin
$\frac{1}{2}$ oz. Dry Vermouth
2 dashes Pernod

PHANTOM MARTINI

Ketel One Vodka
splash Johnny Walker Black Label
Jumbo Black Olive

Morton's "Martini Club"
San Antonio, TX

PICCADILLY COCKTAIL MARTINI

1½ oz. Gin
¾ oz. Dry Vermouth
¼ tsp. Pernod or other
Anise-Flavored Liqueur
¼ tsp. Grenadine

Stir ingredients with ice. Strain into chilled glass.

PICKLED PEPPER MARTINI

2 oz. Absolut Peppar Vodka
splash Pickle Juice

Shake and strain into chilled martini glass. Garnish with thick slice of dill pickle.

PINACRANAKAZE MARTINI

Pineapple infused Skyy Vodka
Lime and Cranberry Juice

Served up in an oversized chilled stem. Shaken, not stirred.
Skyy Martini List

287

PINK DIAMOND MARTINI

    1 part Finlandia Cranberry Vodka
    3 parts Classic Finlandia Vodka
    1 part Peach Schnapps
          Pineapple Juice

Stir gently with ice and strain. Garnish with a perfect maraschino cherry or rose petals floated on top.

PINK MARTINI

    1½ oz. Absolut Vodka
    ½ oz. Cranberry Juice
    dash Dry Vermouth

Garnish with lime squeeze.

Randy Wickstrom
Rainforest
Beach Park, IL

PINK MARTINI TWIST

    Absolut Kurant Vodka
    Chambord

Portland's Best
Portland, OR

PINK POODLE MARTINI

$\frac{3}{4}$ oz. Stoli Cristall Vodka
$\frac{1}{4}$ oz. White Creme de Cacao
$\frac{1}{4}$ oz. Chambord

Mix over ice and strain into chilled
martini glass. Garnish with fresh
raspberry.
Scott DiStefano
Susie's Bar
Calistoga, CA

PINK ROSE

Skyy Vodka
DeKuyper Peachtree
Schnapps
dash Cranberry Juice

Hamiltons
Miami, FL

PINK STINGRAY MARTINI

Finlandia Cranberry Vodka
White Creme de Cacao

Portland's Best
Portland, OR

PINK SWAN COCKTAIL

> Bacardi Añejo Rum
> Cointreau
> Sweet & Sour Mix
> 2 Maraschino cherries

Blend with ice. Rim martini glass
with sugar. Garnish with lime circle,
maraschino cherry and short straws.
Hotel Bel-Air
Los Angeles, CA

PINSK PEACH

Stoli Persik Vodka and Campari
straight up.

PITBULL IN THE SKY

> Skyy Vodka
> splash Grapefruit Juice and a twist

Serve up in an oversized chilled stem.
Shaken, not stirred.
Skyy Martini List

PITBULL MARTINI

> Gordon's Vodka
> splash Grapefruit Juice

Twist.

PLAZA MARTINI

   1½ oz. Bombay Gin
   1½ oz. Martini & Rossi Extra Dry
            Vermouth

Stir in cocktail glass. Strain & serve
straight up or on the rocks. Add lemon
twist or olives.

PLAZA MARTINI II

   1 oz. Dry Gin
   1 oz. Dry Vermouth
   1 oz. Sweet Vermouth
  splash Pineapple Juice

PLYMOUTH COCKTAIL MARTINI

   2½ oz. Dry Gin
  2 dashes Orange Bitters

POET'S DREAM MARTINI

   1 oz. Dry Gin
   ¾ oz. Dry Vermouth
   ¾ oz. Benedictine

Twist of lemon peel.

POINSETTIA MARTINI

   $1\frac{1}{2}$ oz. Absolut Vodka
    $\frac{1}{4}$ oz. Chambord
    $\frac{1}{4}$ oz. Pineapple Juice

Shake with ice and strain into
martini glass.

Linda Bett
Longneckers Saloon
Houston, TX

POLO COCKTAIL MARTINI

   $1\frac{1}{2}$ oz. Gin
    $\frac{3}{4}$ oz. Fresh Orange Juice
    $\frac{1}{2}$ oz. Fresh Lemon Juice

Shake ingredients with ice. Strain
into chilled glass.

POLO MARTINI

   $1\frac{1}{2}$ oz. Vodka
   $1\frac{1}{2}$ oz. Perrier – Jouet Champagne
     dash Peychaud Bitters

Serve up in martini glass. Garnish with
olive and twist on the side.

Windsor Court Hotel
New Orleans, LA

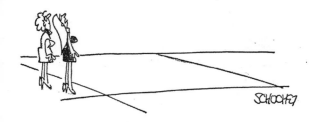

"I DON'T KNOW IF I WANT TO SEE IT.
IT HITS TOO CLOSE TO HOME."

POLO MARTINI CLUB

    1 oz. Dry Gin
    ½ oz. Dry Vermouth
    ⅓ oz. Sweet Vermouth
    ¼ oz. Lime Juice

POLYNESIAN MARTINI

    1½ oz. Smirnoff Vodka
    ¾ oz. Cherry-flavored Brandy
    splash Lime Juice
Chill, strain martini glass with
powdered sugar rim.

POM POM MARTINI

    1½ oz. Dry Vermouth
    ¾ oz. Dry Gin
  2 dashes Orange Bitters

POMEGRANATE MARTINI

Stoli Razberi Vodka shaken with
pomegranate seed & lime.
Lot 61
New York, NY

POO 'TINI'

Clover Honey
Shaken with Belvedere Vodka.
Lot 61
New York, NY

PRESIDENTE MARTINI

1½ oz. Light Rum
½ oz. Dry Vermouth
1 tsp. Triple Sec
1 to 2 dashes Grenadine
Lemon twist

Shake liquid ingredients with cracked ice. Strain into chilled glass. Drop in lemon twist.

PRESIDENTE MARTINI II

1½ oz. Light Rum
¾ oz. Sweet Vermouth
1½ tsp. Dry Vermouth
1 dash Grenadine
Maraschino Cherry

Shake liquid ingredients with cracked ice. Strain into chilled glass. Garnish with maraschino cherry.

PRESSINI

Chilled martini glass. Pour 1 oz.
Pernod. Fill with 2 oz. fresh chilled
espresso. Garnish with 3 white coffee
beans.

NY Steakhouse & Pub
Kearny, NJ

PRINCE'S SMILE MARTINI

2 oz. Gin
1 oz. Apple Brandy
1 oz. Apricot Brandy
½ tsp. Fresh Lemon Juice

Shake ingredients with ice. Strain into
chilled glass. *Prince's Grin: Substitute
apple juice for the Apple Brandy and
apricot nectar for the Apricot Brandy.

PRINCESS MARY

⅓ Cork Dry Gin
⅓ Creme de Cacao
⅓ Fresh Cream

Shake with ice.

PRINCETON MARTINI

  1½ oz. Dry Gin
    1 oz. Port
 2 dashes Orange Bitters
Twist of lemon peel.

PROVINCETOWN-TINI

          Stolichnaya Ohranj Vodka
   splash Finlandia Cranberry Vodka

The Diner on Sycamore
Cincinnati, OH

PSYCHEDELIC MARTINI

  6 parts Dry Gin
  1 part French Vermouth
  1 part Italian Vermouth
  ½ part Orange Juice
  ½ part Pineapple Juice
  1 dash Anisette
Shake.

PUCKERED UP APPLE KISS

DeKuyper Sour Apple
Schnapps
Frozen Vodka

Serve in chilled martini glass.

Hurricane Restaurant
Passagrille, FL

PUMP MARTINI

Olives, lemon twist, or onions
B&B

1½ oz. Vodka
splash Dry Vermouth

In one mixing glass, marinate the olives,
a lemon twist, or onions in B&B. In a
second mixing glass, combine Vodka,
Vermouth, and several ice cubes. Stir
and strain into a chilled martini glass.
Garnish with the marinated olives,
lemon twist, or onions.

The Pump Room
Chicago, IL

PUNT E MES NEGRONI
   ¾ oz. Dry Gin
   ¾ oz. Sweet Vermouth
   ¾ oz. Punt e Mes
Twist of lemon peel.

PURE MARTINI
   2 oz. Bombay Sapphire Gin
   1 tsp. Noilly Prat Dry Vermouth
     2 Spanish cocktail olives for
        garnish
In a shaker half-filled with ice, combine
Gin and Vermouth. Shake well, and
strain into a chilled martini glass.
Garnish with olives skewered on a pick.
The Ritz-Carlton Bar
San Francisco, CA

PURE PRECIPITATION MARTINI
   2 oz. Rain Vodka chilled
Strain into martini glass. Garnish with
slice of orange.

PURE ROYALTY MARTINI

Royalty Vodka
Dry Vermouth
Garnish with a lemon twist.
The Martini Bar
Chianti Restaurant
Houston, TX

PURITAN MARTINI

1¾ oz. Dry Gin
½ oz. Dry Vermouth
¼ oz. Yellow Chartreuse
1 dash Orange Bitters

PURPLE HAZE MARTINI

Pint glass filled with ice.
2½ oz. Vodka
½ oz. Raspberry
Liqueur/Chambord
2 oz. Sweet & Sour
splash 7-Up
Shake and serve with strainer and
martini glass.
Robert Lehmann
The Broadway Grill
Seattle, WA

PURPLE HAZE MARTINI II

 ½ oz. Vodka
 ½ oz. Chambord
 dash Triple Sec
 splash Lime Juice
 splash Soda Water

PURPLE HOOTER MARTINI

 ¼ shot Chambord
 ¼ shot Vodka
 ¼ shot Sour Mix
 ¼ shot Lemon-Lime Soda
Chill.

PURPLE MARTINI

 4 oz. Grey Goose Vodka
 splash Elysium
Mario Arredondo of Biba
Boston, MA

PURPLE MASK

 1½ oz. Smirnoff Vodka
 1 oz. Grape Juice
 splash White Creme de Cacao
Chill and strain into chilled martini
glass.

PURPLE PEOPLE EATER

    2 oz. Bacardi Limón
    3 oz. Cranberry Juice
  dribble Blue Curacao
   splash Martini & Rossi Extra Dry
           Vermouth

Shake with ice. Strain into chilled glasses.

PURPLE RAIN MARTINI

  1 part Rain Vodka chilled
  1 part Chambord chilled

Strain into martini glass. Garnish with twist of lime.

Rain Vodka
New Orleans, LA

PURPLETINI

    2 oz. Absolut Kurant
   ½ oz. Chambord
   ½ oz. Triple Sec

Garnish with lemon twist.

Mark Prouty
Ground Round
Framingham, MA

QUATRINI MARTINI

Chocolate martini garnished with chocolate pennies.

Lot 61
New York, NY

QUEEN ELIZABETH MARTINI

1½ oz. Bombay Gin
dash Martini & Rossi Extra Dry
Vermouth

Add splash Benedictine. Stir in cocktail glass. Strain & serve straight up or on the rocks. Add lemon twist or olives.

QUEEN MARTINI

2 parts Dry Gin
1 part Italian Vermouth
1 part French Vermouth
1 dash Orange Bitters
1 dash Angostura Bitters

QUEENIE-TINI

Absolut Kurant Vodka
Chambord
Champagne

The Diner on Sycamore
Cincinnati, OH

R & R MARTINI
1½ oz. Gordon's Vodka
dash Aquavit

R.A.C.
2 oz. Cork Dry Gin
¼ oz. Dry Vermouth
1 Maraschino Cherry and twist
of Orange
dash Orange Bitters
dash Grenadine
Mix.

RACQUET CLUB MARTINI
1¾ oz. Dry Gin
¾ oz. Dry Vermouth
1 dash Orange Bitters
Orange peel

RADARTINI
2 parts Smirnoff Vodka
1 part Tomato Juice
Olive
The Windsock Bar & Grill
San Diego, CA

RAGAZZI CHE MARTINI

        2 oz. Belvedere Vodka
    1/4 oz. Godiva Liqueur
    1/4 oz. Apricot Brandy
              Grapefruit juice

MAD 28
New York, NY

RAIDME MARTINI

    1 3/4 oz. Dry Gin
      1/2 oz. Pernod
      1/4 oz. Campari

RAINFOREST
MARTINI

    1 part Rain Vodka chilled
    1 part Midori Melon Liqueur
    splash 7-Up

Strain into martini glass. Garnish with
twist of lime.
Rain Vodka
New Orleans, LA

RAINIER MARTINI

    12 Sour Cherries
1 oz. Belvedere Vodka
    1 Calvados-marinated cherry

Combine sour cherries with the Vodka and let stand 24 hours. Stir well with ice and strain into an ice cold martini glass. Garnish with the Calvados-marinated Bing cherry.

Garden Court at the Four Seasons
Olympic Hotel
Seattle, WA

RAIN LOVE MARTINI

1 oz. Rain Vodka
½ oz. White Creme de Cacao
¼ oz. Chambord

Chill and serve in classic martini glass.

Marcovaldo Dionysas, Bartender
Absinthe Bar & Restaurant
San Francisco, CA

RANCH STYLE MARTINI

Vodka or Gin
Patron Tequila

Serve with a pickled olive.

Sheraton Seattle
Seattle, WA

RASBERTINI

> Stoli Razberi Vodka
> dash Stoli Ohranj Vodka

Orange slice garnish.
Renaissance Atlanta Hotel
Atlanta, GA

RASCHOCOLATE MARTINI

1½ oz. Smirnoff Vodka
1 oz. White Creme de Cacao
dash Raspberry Liqueur
2 oz. Cranberry Juice

Chill and strain into chilled martini glass.

RASPBERRY CHOCOLATE MARTINI

1½ oz. Chambord
1½ oz. White Creme de Cacao

Shake, top with raspberry. Serve straight up or on the rocks.
Joseph Vuckovic
Russo's on the Bay
Howard Beach, NY

RASPBERRY MARTINI

    1 part Godiva Liqueur
    1 part Absolut Vodka
    splash Chambord

Combine with ice and shake well. Serve in a glass whose rim has been dipped in powdered sugar.

RASPBERRY MARTINI II

    $\frac{1}{2}$ oz. Monin Raspberry Syrup
    $1\frac{1}{2}$ oz. Gin or Vodka

Pour over ice. Garnish with lemon twist or olive.
Monin Special Cocktail Recipes

RASPBERRY MARTINI III

    2 oz. Smirnoff Vodka
    splash Raspberry Liqueur

Chill, strain and top with fresh raspberries.

"THE MARTINIS ARE READY."

RASPBERRY TRUFFLE

    1 shot Tanqueray Sterling Vodka
    ½ oz. Baileys Irish Cream
    ½ oz. Kahlua
    ½ oz. Chambord
    mist Martini & Rossi Extra Dry
          Vermouth

Shake. Serve in iced martini glass.
Garnish with Cocoa Powder on the
rim of the glass, a chocolate stick and
raspberry.

RASPBERRY TWIST MARTINI

    1½ oz. Ketel One Vodka
    ¼ oz. Chambord
          Bonny Doon Framboise
          infusion (local product)
          Fresh Raspberries

Polo Lounge
Windsor Court Hotel
New Orleans, LA

RASPBERRY VODKA MARTINI

  2 oz. Stoli Razberi Vodka
  splash Chambord Liqueur

Shake with ice and strain into chilled martini glass. Garnish with lime twist.

Jason Wingerter
Peroni Waterfront Restaurant

RATTLER MARTINI

  ¾ oz. Dry Gin
  ¾ oz. French Vermouth
  ¾ oz. Italian Vermouth
  ½ oz. Orange Juice

RATTLESNAKE MARTINI

  2 oz. Stoli Cristall Vodka
  ¼ oz. Chambord
  2 splashes Cranberry Juice
  1 splash Pineapple Juice
  squeeze Lemon & Lime

Shake and serve up with a twist.

Bobby Carroll
Rattlesnake Bar & Grill
Boston, MA

RAZZLE DAZZLE
 1 oz. Stoli Razberi Vodka
 splash Chambord
Garnish with lemon twist.
Peggy Howell
Cotati Yacht Club & Saloon
Cotati, CA

REAL GORDON'S MARTINI
 Gordon's Vodka
 Dry Vermouth
 Lemon twist

RED APPLE MARTINI
 ¾ oz. Dry Gin
 ¾ oz. Sweet Vermouth
 ½ oz. Apple Brandy
 ½ oz. Grenadine

RE-BAR RED
 2 oz. Campari
 Juice of two Lime Wedges
 Juice of two Lemon Wedges
 splash 7-up

RED GIN-GIN MARTINI

   Dry Vermouth
 3 oz. Gin
 1 oz. Sloe Gin
 1 spiral Orange twist for garnish

Stir with ice and strain into chilled
martini glass. Garnish with spiral
orange twist.

The Mandarin
San Francisco, CA

RED-HOT MARTINI

Vodka, Cinnamon Schnapps with a
hint of Romana Sambuca, served with
Red Hots.

RED MARTINI

 2 oz. Beefeater Gin
 $1/10$ oz. Dry Vermouth
  dash Campari

Shake over ice and strain into a chilled
martini glass. Garnish with a lemon.

RED MARTINI II

    dash Grenadine
1½ oz. Gin
 ½ oz. Dry Vermouth
 ½ oz. Sloe Gin

RED NUT

        Stoli Vodka
splash Frangelico
Hotel San Remo
Las Vegas, NV

RED PASSION MARTINI

1½ oz. Alizé
 ½ oz. Campari
Stir well and serve like a martini.
Garnish with orange peel.

RED RIM MARTINI

Rim glass with Sweet Vermouth. Dip
rim in red sugar. Add: 1 oz. Gordon's
Vodka, 1½ oz. raspberry-white grape
juice. Blackberry garnish.

RED ROOM MARTINI

    4 oz. Stoli Razberi Vodka
    1 oz. Alizé Red Passion
  splash Sour Mix
Shake and serve with twist.
Bob Albright
Le Cirque 2000
New York, NY

RED ROYAL MARTINI

          Crown Royal Whiskey
          Amaretto
Portland's Best
Portland, OR

REDWOOD ROOM MARTINI

    3 oz. Grey Goose Vodka
       3 Olives, one stuffed with
          Gorgonzola cheese
1 eye drop Vermouth
Joe Watts
The Clift Hotel's Redwood Room
San Francisco, CA

REEBOK MARTINI

　2½ oz.　Skyy Vodka
　½ oz.　Peach Schnapps
　½ oz.　Martini & Rossi Extra Dry
　　　　　Vermouth

Lemon twist soaked in Grand Marnier.
Reebok Sports Clubs

REFORM COCKTAIL MARTINI

　1½ oz.　Dry Sherry
　¾ oz.　Dry Vermouth
　1 dash　Orange Bitters
　　　　　Maraschino Cherry

Stir liquid ingredients with ice. Strain
into chilled glass. Garnish with
maraschino cherry.

RENDEZVOUS MARTINI

　1½ oz.　Dry Gin
　½ oz.　Kirschwasser
　¼ oz.　Campari

Twist of Lemon peel.

RICHMOND MARTINI
1¾ oz. Dry Gin
¾ oz. Lillet
Twist of lemon peel.

RISING SUN MARTINI
Skyy Vodka
mist Grand Marnier
Orange twist
Serve up in an oversized chilled stem.
Shaken, not stirred.

ROBIN'S NEST
1½ oz. Smirnoff Vodka
1 oz. Cranberry Juice
splash White Creme de Cacao
Chill and strain into martini glass.

ROBYN'S BLUE BOMBER
2 oz. Beefeater Gin
1 drop Dry Vermouth
¼ oz. Blue Curacao
In iced shaker, shake and strain in
chilled martini glass.
Robyn Suchowski
Elizabeth, NJ

ROCKEFELLER

        Hennessey V.S.
        Stoli Cristall Vodka
        Champagne
        Lemon twist

Coat inside of chilled martini glass with Hennessey, discard excess. Mix Stoli in a shaker and stir. Add cold champagne just before straining into glass. Garnish with lemon twist.

Matthew Milani
Pittsburgh, PA

ROLLS ROYCE MARTINI

    2 oz. Dry Gin
    1 oz. Sweet Vermouth
    $1/2$ oz. Benedictine
    $1/2$ oz. Dry Vermouth

Shake and strain.

ROMA MARTINI
  1½ oz. Dry Gin
   ½ oz. Sweet Vermouth
   ½ oz. Dry Vermouth
     3 Fresh Strawberries

ROSA MARTINI
  1½ oz. Bombay Gin
   dash Martini & Rossi Extra Dry
           Vermouth
Add Hiram Walker Cherry Flavored
Brandy. Stir in cocktail glass. Strain &
serve straight up or on the rocks. Add
lemon twist or olives.

ROSALIN RUSSELL MARTINI
  1½ oz. Bombay Gin
   dash Aquavit
Stir in cocktail glass. Strain & serve
straight up or on the rocks. Add lemon
twist or olives.

ROSE du BOY

    1½ oz. Dry Gin
    ½ oz. Dry Vermouth
    ¼ oz. Cherry-flavored Brandy
    ¼ oz. Kirschwasser

ROSE KENNEDY MARTINI

    1½ oz. Vodka
    1 oz. Peach Schnapps
    3 oz. Lemonade (preferably fresh
         squeezed)
  splash Cranberry Juice

Fill blender with ice; add all ingredients.
Blend and pour into glass. Garnish with
lime wedge.

Patrick Ford
Smith & Wollensky's
New York, NY

ROSE MARIE MARTINI

    1¼ oz. Dry Gin
    ½ oz. Dry Vermouth
    ¼ oz. Armagnac
    ¼ oz. Cherry-flavored Brandy
    ¼ oz. Campari

ROSE PETAL

>   Belvedere Vodka
>   Grand Marnier
>   Martini & Rossi Extra Dry
>   Vermouth

Garnish with real Rose petals.

Iggy's
Chicago, IL

ROSELYN MARTINI

1½ oz. Bombay Gin
   dash Martini & Rossi Extra Dry
         Vermouth

Add Rose's Grenadine. Stir in cocktail glass. Strain & serve straight up or on the rocks. Add lemon twist or olives.

ROSE'S MARTINI

1½ oz. Absolut Vodka
 splash Rose's Lime Juice
 splash Chambord

Mix in shaker glass with ice. Strain into martini glass. Serve with a lime.

Donna Eldridge, Bar Manager
Spuds Restaurant & Pub
Danvers, MA

ROYAL COCKTAIL MARTINI
1¾ oz. Dry Gin
¾ oz. Dubonnet
1 dash Orange Bitters
1 dash Angostura Bitters

ROYAL DEVIL
Stoli Razberi Vodka
Chambord
Black Haus Liqueur
Served chilled and straight up.

ROYAL ROMANCE
1½ oz. Cork Dry Gin
¼ oz. Grand Marnier
½ oz. Passion Fruit Juice
1 dash Sugar Syrup

ROYAL WEDDING MARTINI
Tanqueray Gin or Stolichnaya Vodka.
Handsomely married to a dash of
Chivas Regal.
Oliver's Mayflower Park Hotel
Seattle, WA

RUBY SLIPPER MARTINI

    2 oz. Bombay Sapphire
    1/4 oz. Grand Marnier
    1 or 2 splashes of Grenadine
    1 dash Peppermint Schnapps
Garnish with a mint leaf (set it
on the edge of the drink and let it
stick out).

RUM MARTINI

    5 parts Light Rum
    1 part French Vermouth
Twist of lemon peel.

RUNYONS MARTINI

    3 oz. Stoli Ohranj Vodka
    1 dash Dry Vermouth
Stirred over ice. Served straight up in a
chilled martini glass. Garnish with a
slice of orange.

RUSKI LIMONNADE

    1 oz. Stoli Limonnaya Vodka
   splash Simple Syrup
Garnish with lemon twist.
Peggy Howell
Cotati Yacht Club & Saloon
Cotati, CA

RUSSIAN BRUSHFIRE

        Stoli Pertsovka Vodka
  1 dash Tabasco sauce
     part Bloody Mary Mix
  1 mini Jalapeño Pepper
Mix Stoli and small portion of Bloody
Mary mix with ice. (enough to make
drink red in color). Shake and strain
into chilled martini glass. Garnish with
pepper and dash of Tabasco.
Matthew Milani
Pittsburgh, PA

RUSSIAN DELIGHT MARTINI

Stoli Vanil Vodka with splash of
DiSaronno Amaretto chilled.

325

RUSSIAN MALTED MARTINI

    2 oz. Stoli Cristall Vodka
    1/4 oz. Lagavulin (or comparable
            single malt scotch)

Garnish with a twist.

RUSSIAN MARTINI

    3/4 oz. Stoli Vodka
    3/4 oz. Gin
    3/4 oz. White Creme de Cacao

Chill, strain and serve in a chilled martini glass.

RUSSIAN MARTINI II

         Stoliychnaya Ohranj Vodka
         Champagne
         Orange Zest

Martini's
New York, NY

RUSSIAN TIRAMISU

         Stoli Kafya & Stoli Vanil
         Vodka

S'MORE MARTINI
Martini glass rim dipped in cinnamon.
> Finlandia Vodka
> Chocolate Liqueur
> Martini & Rossi Rosso
> Vermouth

SAKE MARTINI
> Belvedere Vodka Shaken with
> a dash of Sake & Gin

Garnished with a cucumber.

SAKE MARTINI II
> Stoli Ohranj Vodka
> splash Dry Sake

Cucumber slice garnish.

SAKITINI MARTINI
> 1½ oz. Bombay Gin
> dash Sake

Stir in cocktail glass. Strain & serve
straight up or on the rocks. Add lemon
twist or olives.

SAKITINI MARTINI II

    1½ oz. Smirnoff Vodka at room
              temperature
top with 2½ oz. Hot Sake
Garnish with pickled Ginger and a
dollop of Wasabi.

SALOME MARTINI

    1 oz. Dry Gin
    ¾ oz. Dry Vermouth
    ¾ oz. Dubonnet

SALT N' PEPPER

Absolut Peppar Vodka martini with
cocktail onions. Serve in chilled glass
with salted rim.
Cecilia's
Breckenridge, CO

SAM I AM MARTINI

    1¼ oz. Absolut Citron Vodka
    ¼ oz. Amaretto
    3 oz. Cranberry Juice
Shake and serve up in martini glass
with twist of lemon.
Sambonn Lek, Head Bartender
Renaissance Mayflower Hotel
Washington, DC

SAN FRANCISCO
COCKTAIL MARTINI

    3/4 oz. Sloe Gin
    3/4 oz. Dry Vermouth
    3/4 oz. Sweet Vermouth
    1 dash Angostura Bitters
    1 dash Orange Bitters
                Maraschino Cherry

Shake liquid ingredients with ice. Strain into chilled glass. Drop in maraschino cherry.

SAN MARTIN MARTINI

    3/4 oz. Dry Gin
    3/4 oz. Dry Vermouth
    3/4 oz. Sweet Vermouth
    1/4 oz. Anisette
    1 dash Bitters

SANGRIA MARTINI (SANGRATINI)

2 oz.	Vodka (Stoli Ohranj or Smirnoff Citrus twist)
½ oz.	Dry Red Wine (Cabernet Sauvignon, or Merlot)
½ oz.	Orange Juice
1 dash	Brandy (optional)
1 dash	Rose's Lime Juice

Big squeeze of lemon, and the same of lime. Shake or stir with lots of fresh ice, then strain into a martini glass. Garnish with an orange slice.

SAPPHIRE MARTINI

Bombay Sapphire Gin
Cinzano Vermouth

Garnish with an olive.

SAPPHIRE MARTINI II

Bombay Sapphire
Pearl Onions

Polo Lounge
Windsor Court Hotel
New Orleans, LA

SARATOGA MARTINI

  1½ oz. Smirnoff Vodka
2 dashes Grenadine
2 dashes Angostura Bitters
  splash Soda Water
Garnish with pineapple wedge.

SARGASSO MARTINI

  2 oz. Skyy Vodka
¼ oz. Midori
¼ oz. Blue Curacao
Garnish with lime twist.

SASSY JO

        Bombay Gin
        Sweet & Dry Vermouths
  splash OJ and Bitters
Brasserie Jo Martini's
Chicago, IL

SATAN'S WHISKERS

½ oz. Gin
½ oz. Dry Vermouth
¼ oz. Sweet Vermouth
½ oz. Orange Juice
¼ oz. Grand Marnier
dash Orange Bitters or Orange twists

Shake and strain into cocktail glass.
Garnish with orange slice and red
maraschino cherry.

Charlie Chop
US Bartenders' Guild
Los Angeles, CA

SAUZA BREEZE MARTINI

Sauza Tequila
Chambord
Sour Mix and Lime

Gatsby
Boca Raton, FL

SAVOY HOTEL SPECIAL MARTINI

1½ oz. Dry Gin
½ oz. Dry Vermouth
1 dash Pernod
2 dashes Grenadine
Twist of lemon peel.

SAVOY MARTINI

1¾ oz. Dry Gin
½ oz. Dry Vermouth
¼ oz. Dubonnet
Orange peel

SAVOY MARTINI II

Infuse Smirnoff Vodka with
Ripe Bartlett Pears
2 oz. Infused Smirnoff Vodka
Chill, strain and garnish with a fresh
pear slice.

SCARLETTINI

Ketel One Vodka
A touch of Bonny Doon's
Raspberry Wine
Glenn's Restaurant & Cool Bar
Newburyport, MA

SCHNOZZLE MARTINI

¾ oz. Dry Gin
¾ oz. Dry Vermouth
½ oz. Cocktail Sherry
¼ oz. Pernod
¼ oz. Orange Curacao

SCOTLAND YARD MARTINI

Tanqueray
splash Scotch

No. 18
New York, NY

SEA SPRAY MARTINI

Leyden Dry Gin
Midori Melon Liqueur
Pineapple Juice

Red Lobster
Memphis, TN

SEAN LAPP MARTINI

Tanqueray Sterling Vodka
Blue Cheese Olives
Onion Olives

Yvette Wintergarden
Chicago, IL

SEDUCTION MARTINI

Combine 1 1/2 oz. Smirnoff Vodka with
a splash of Brandy and Benedictine.
1/3 oz. bar lime, splash of Grenadine.
Strain and garnish with orange wheel.

SEED N ZEST TINI

Fennel seed. Orange zest freshly ground
and shaken with Belvedere Vodka.

Lot 61
New York, NY

SELF-STARTER MARTINI

1½ oz.	Dry Gin
¾ oz.	Lillet
¼ oz.	Apricot-flavored Brandy
2 dashes	Pernod

SEVENTH HEAVEN MARTINI

1½ oz.	Gin
½ oz.	Maraschino Cherry Juice
½ oz.	Unsweetened Grapefruit Juice
	Mint sprig

Shake liquid ingredients with ice. Strain
into chilled glass. Drop in orange twist.

SEVENTH REGIMENT MARTINI

1¾ oz.	Dry Gin
¾ oz.	Sweet Vermouth
2 twists	Lemon Peel

Stir twists with drink.

SEXUAL TRANCE
MARTINI

  Absolut Citron Vodka
  Midori
  Chambord
  Orange Juice
  Pineapple Juice
  Sweet & Sour

Garnish with a maraschino cherry.

SEXY DEVIL

2 parts Finlandia Vodka
1 part Finlandia Cranberry Vodka
  (Infused with fresh
  strawberries)
dash Martini & Rossi Extra Dry
  Vermouth

Garnish with lemon peel wrapped
"Holland" pepper.

Centro Ristorante
Chicago, IL

SHAKEN NOT STIRRED MARTINI

Tanqueray Gin
Ketel One Vodka
Lillet
Lemon twist

Yvette Wintergarden
Chicago, IL

SHAMPOO FOR THE BEAUTIFUL

2 parts Martini & Rossi Dry Vermouth
1 part Vodka
3 parts Champagne

Serve in long glass with plenty of ice.

Raymond Taylor
Kent, UK

SHARKBITE MARTINI

Leyden Dry Gin
Sprite
squeeze Lemon

Red Lobster
Memphis, TN

SHARP SUSIE MARTINI

>   1 part Finlandia Arctic Cranberry
>   Vodka
>   1 part Absolut Kurant Vodka
>   1 part Absolut Citron Vodka
>   1 part Cointreau

Shake well and pour into an ice cold cocktail glass. Garnish with a pearl onion.

Krisu
E-mail

SHERRY COCKTAIL MARTINI

>   2 oz. Dry Sherry
>   1/2 oz. Dry Vermouth
> 2 dashes Orange Bitters

SHISO & LIME LEAF MARTINI

Muddle 3 lime leaves & 2 Shiso leaves with a large dash of sugar syrup. Add a large pour of Ketel One Vodka. Shake well. Strain through martini glass. Garnish with one Shiso & one Lime leaf in the martini glass.

Lot 61
Ben Pundole, General Manager
New York, NY

SIFI FLIP

    1 oz. Cork Dry Gin
    ¼ oz. Cointreau
    ¼ oz. Grenadine
           Juice of ½ Lemon
           Yolk of Egg

Shake and strain.

SILK PANTIES MARTINI

Smooth blend of Stoli Vodka and Peach Schnapps.

SILK SPIRIT

    1 oz. Stoli Vanil Vodka
    ½ oz. Wild Spirit
    ¼ oz. Chocolate Liqueur

Served chilled and straight up.

SILKEN VEIL MARTINI

    1 oz. Vodka
    1 oz. Dubonnet Rouge

Chill, strain and garnish with a lemon twist.

SILVER BIKINI MARTINI
Pour 2 oz. Gordon's Orange Vodka
into martini shaker. Add splash of
Framboise. Fill shaker with ice, shake
and strain into martini glass. Garnish
with raspberry.

SILVER BULLET MARTINI
1½ oz. Bombay Gin
  dash Martini & Rossi Extra Dry
        Vermouth
Shake, strain & serve up or on the rocks
with some ice. Float J&B Scotch on top.

SILVER STREAK MARTINI
1½ oz. Dry Gin
1½ oz. Kummel
Pour over finely crushed ice in small
wine glass.

"THE OLIVE HAS DROPPED!"

SIMPSON MARTINI

    2 oz. Vodka
    ¾ oz. Vermouth over ice and
             shake well

Pour into traditional martini glass.
Garnish with: sliver of orange peel,
black olive speared with dagger plastic
toothpick.
Karen Pike Davis
Easton, PA

SKYY BLUE BUDDHA

    2 oz. Skyy Vodka
    ¼ oz. Sake
    ¼ oz. Grapefruit Juice
    ¼ oz. Blue Curacao
    ½ oz. Lemon Juice
    ½ oz. Lime Juice
  splash Simple Syrup

Garnish with fresh orange slice.
301 Sake Bar and Restaurant
San Francisco, CA

SKYY MARTINI

2½ oz. Skyy Vodka
splash Blue Curacao

Shake over ice and strain into well
chilled glass. Garnish with 2 olives.

The Boulder's Inn
Roxbury, CT

SKYY HIGH MARTINI

2 oz. Skyy Vodka
¼ oz. Martini & Rossi Dry
Vermouth

Shake with ice and strain into a martini
glass with a jumbo olive.

Heart & Soul
San Francisco, CA

SKYY HIGH MARTINI II

Skyy Vodka
Raspberry Liqueur
Lemon twist

The Windsock Bar & Grill
San Diego, CA

SKYY WHITE CHOCOLATE MARTINI

Skyy Vodka

White Creme de Cacao

Serve up in an oversized chilled stem glass. Shaken, not stirred.

Skyy Martini List

SKYY-FI MARTINI

2½ oz. Skyy Vodka

½ oz. Midori

½ oz. Blue Curacao

Chilled and served straight up with lemon twist.

Diane Moscato
7 Central Public House
Manchester, MA

SLOE VERMOUTH MARTINI

1 oz. Sloe Gin

1 oz. Dry Vermouth

2 tsp. Fresh Lemon Juice

Shake ingredients with ice. Strain into chilled glass.

SMASHED PUMPKIN

    1 oz. Godiva Liqueur

    ½ oz. Godet White Chocolate
                 Liqueur

    ½ oz. Cointreau

    ½ oz. Grey Goose Vodka

Garnish with chocolate orange slice.

Jill Ruggles and Erica Holm
Drink
Chicago, IL

SMILER MARTINI

    1¼ oz. Dry Gin

    ½ oz. Dry Vermouth

    ½ oz. Sweet Vermouth

    ¼ oz. Orange Juice

    1 dash Angostura Bitters

Shake.

SMIRNOFF NUTCRACKER MARTINI

    2 oz. Smirnoff Vodka

    ½ oz. Almond Liqueur

Chill, strain and serve in a martini glass.
Garnish with almonds.

SMOKEY MARTINI

Tanqueray Gin
Scotch
Lemon twist

Yvette Wintergarden
Chicago, IL

SMOKEY MARTINI II

Coat a martini glass with a good whiskey, discard excess. Make a normal Vodka Martini (shaken not stirred); add to glass.

Mark Wijman, Almere
The Netherlands

SMOKEY MOUNTAIN MARTINI

1$\frac{1}{2}$ oz. Finlandia Vodka
$\frac{1}{4}$ oz. Knob Creek Bourbon

Shake and strain into martini glass.

Brett Egan, Director
National Bartenders School
Lakewood, CA

SMOOTH OPERATOR
  2 oz. OP.
  ½ oz. Irish Cream
  ½ oz. Coffee Liqueur
  ½ oz. White Creme de Menthe
Shake with ice. Serve on the rocks or in
a martini glass.

SMOOTH MARTINI
        Ketel One Vodka
Fill shaker with half ice cubes and half
shaved ice. Shake and strain into chilled
martini glass.

SNOWBALL MARTINI
  1½ oz. Gin
  ½ oz. Pernod or other Anise-
          Flavored Liqueur
  ½ oz. Cream
Shake ingredients with ice. Strain into
chilled glass.

SNOWCONE MARTINI

 1 oz. Bacardi Spice Rum
 1 oz. Banana Liqueur
 ½ oz. Blue Curacao
mist of Martini & Rossi Extra Dry
    Vermouth

Garnish with a large ball of ice in the
middle of the cocktail.

Michael Jordans
Chicago, IL

SNYDER MARTINI

 1¾ oz. Dry Gin
 ½ oz. Dry Vermouth
 ¼ oz. Orange Curacao
    Orange peel

SO-CO-MARTINI

 2 oz. Southern Comfort
 ¼ oz. Sweet Vermouth
 ¼ oz. Dry Vermouth
    Maraschino Cherry

No. 18
New York, NY

SOLAR FLARE MARTINI

1½ oz. Tanqueray Gin
¼ oz. Dry Vermouth

Shake & strain. 5 drops of Creme de
Noyaux. Garnish maraschino cherry
with stem.

Doug Bravo
Texas Station Hotel & Casino
Las Vegas, NV

SOME LIKE IT HOT MARTINI

2 oz. Absolut Peppar Vodka
Red Chili Pepper

Yvette Wintergarden
Chicago, IL

SOME MOTHER MARTINI

1¾ oz. Dry Gin
½ oz. Dry Vermouth
¼ oz. Pernod

Cocktail onion.

SONIC GOLD MARTINI

    1½ oz. Stolichnaya Gold Vodka
    1½ oz. Campari
    splash Cranberry Juice
    splash Tonic
             Soda water to fill glass
             Orange Slice

Pour all ingredients, except soda water over ice in a tall glass. Fill rest of the glass with soda water. Stir and garnish with orange slice.

C3 Restaurant & Lounge
New York, NY

SOPRANO

    2 oz. OP.
    ¼ oz. Dry Vermouth
    float Sambuca on top

Serve on the rocks.

SOPRANO ROYAL

    2 oz. OP.
    ¼ oz. Campari

Shake with ice. Serve up or on the rocks.

SOUR APPLE MARTINI

    2 oz. Grey Goose Vodka
    1/2 oz. Apple Pucker Schnapps
Garnish with slice of Granny Smith
Apple.
Michael Waller
Martini's
San Francisco, CA

SOUR KISSES MARTINI

    1 1/2 oz. Bombay Gin
    dash Martini & Rossi Extra Dry
            Vermouth
Add egg white. Strain & serve straight
up or on the rocks. Add lemon twist or
olive.

SOUR PATCH MARTINI

    2 oz. each Stoli Ohranj, Razberi,
            Strasberi Vodka
    splash Pineapple, Sour Mix, Orange
            Juice and Grenadine
Gatsby
Boca Raton, FL

SOUTH BEACH

 2 oz. Bacardi Rum
 ½ oz. Malibu
 ½ oz. Pineapple Juice
 ¼ oz. Blue Curacao

Gatsby
Boca Raton, FL

SOUTHERN GIN
COCKTAIL MARTINI

 2¼ oz. Dry Gin
 ¼ oz. Orange Curacao
 2 dashes Orange Bitters

SOVIET MARTINI

 2 oz. Smirnoff Vodka
 ½ oz. Sherry
 splash Dry Vermouth

Chill, strain and garnish with a lemon
twist.

SOVIET SLUSH

2 parts	Stoli Ohranj Vodka
1 part	Gin
1 part	Rumple Minze
1 part	Black Haus Blackberry Schnapps
2 scoops	Rainbow Sherbet

Mix in blender and serve in hurricane glass. Garnish with piece of kiwi fruit and mint leaf.

Eric Morris
Mulligans
Salisbury, MD

SPANISH MARTINI

½ oz.	Dry Sack Sherry
1½ oz.	Gin
1 twist	Lemon

Blend & stir.

SPICED OYSTER MARTINI

Fresh Kumamoto Oyster covered with jalepeño, Tabasco, Lemon juice, and Frozen Belvedere Vodka.

Lot 61
New York, NY

SPICY HARD SHELL FAVORITE

1½ oz. Stoli Pertsovka Vodka, 3 dashes
Texas Pete hot sauce.

Jeff McCarthy
The Hard Shell
Richmond, VA

SPHINX MARTINI

2 oz.	Beefeater Gin
¼ oz.	Sweet Vermouth
¾ oz.	Dry Vermouth
	Lemon Wedge

SPIAGGI

Stolichnaya Vanil Vodka
Tuaca Italian Liqueur

Maureen & Stephen Horn
Mermaid Martini Bar, Spiaggi
Cape May, NJ

ST. TROPEZ MARTINI

1½ oz.	Smirnoff Vodka
splash	Peach Schnapps
splash	Orange Juice
dash	Grenadine

Chill, strain and garnish with a fresh
peach wedge.

STAKE MARTINI

Vodka shaken with a dash of Sake &
Gin. Garnished with cucumber.

Lot 61
New York, NY

STANG BILL MARTINI

$1\frac{1}{2}$ oz. Tanqueray Gin poured into glass
shaker with ice. Wash martini glass with
The Famous Grouse. Roll shaker with Gin
back and forth mixing Gin into ice. Top
shaker with ice and strain Gin into glass
using ice as strainer. Garnish with olives.

Bill Stang, Bartender
The Blackduck Freehouse
Saskatchewan, BC

STAR COCKTAIL MARTINI

$1\frac{1}{2}$ oz. Apple Brandy
$1\frac{1}{2}$ oz. Sweet Vermouth
2 dashes Angostura Bitters
          Lemon twist

Stir liquid ingredients with ice. Strain
into chilled glass. Drop in lemon twist.

STARRY NIGHT

    2 oz. Vincent Vodka
    ½ oz. Blue Curacao
    splash Sweet & Sour Mix

Combine ingredients and pour into a martini glass. Garnish with lemon twist.

Andy Porter
Van Gogh's Restaurant & Bar
Atlanta, GA

STAR TINI

Rinse glass with Martini & Rossi Extra Dry Vermouth

    2½ oz. Stoli Crystall Vodka
    ½ oz. Campari

Orange twist to garnish.

Harry Denton's Starlight Room
San Francisco, CA

STARBURST MARTINI

    2 oz. Grey Goose Vodka
    1 oz. Strawberry Liqueur
    ½ oz. Pineapple Juice
    ½ oz. Sour Mix
    pinch Sugar

Mix all ingredients and shake vigorously. Serve with a strawberry.

"Smiley" of Bash Nightclub
Miami, FL

"SURE, HE'S A MERRY OL' SOUL,
SO WOULD YOU BE, IF YOU
WALKED AROUND ALL DAY SIPPING
A VODKA MARTINI."

STARLIGHT MARTINI

  1¾ oz. Beefeater Gin
   ¾ oz. Orange Curacao
  1 dash Angostura Bitters
Shake.

STARTINI

Rinse glass with Dry Vermouth
     2 oz. Belvedere Vodka
few drops Edmond Briottet
           Mandarin Liqueur
Stirred, not shaken. Garnish with
Orange Zest.
Jeramiah Tower's Stars Restaurant
San Francisco, CA

STEFANO MARTINI

  1½ oz. Smirnoff Vodka
   float Lemonade
   dash Grenadine
Chill and strain into a martini glass.

STERLING GOLD MARTINI

       Tanqueray Sterling Vodka
  touch Tuaca and a zest of orange
Oliver's Mayflower Park Hotel
Seattle, WA

STICK 'EM UP
Equal parts Cactus Juice Liqueur and Vodka.

STILL LIFE MARTINI
2 oz. Smirnoff Vodka
¼ oz. Coffee Liqueur
¼ oz. Baileys Irish Cream
Strain and garnish with an orange wheel and maraschino cherry.

STOLI BELLINI MARTINI
Champagne
Stoli Persik Vodka
splash Peach Schnapps

STOLI BIKINI MARTINI
Pour 3 oz. of Stoli Ohranj Vodka into martini shaker. Add generous splash of Framboise. Fill shaker with ice and shake or stir vigorously. Strain liquid into martini glasses. Garnish with raspberry.

STOLI GRAND MARTINI

2 oz. Dry Vermouth in tumbler
with crushed ice

Drain off Vermouth. Pour in 1½ oz. Stoli
Ohranj Vodka. ¼ oz. Grand Marnier. Swirl
in tumbler for 2-3 minutes until silky.

Jay Tarantino
Taverne on the Lake
Lawrenceburg, IN

STOLI HUMMER

1 oz. Stoli Vanil Vodka
1 oz. Amaretto
1 oz. Bacardi Rum
½ oz. Grenadine
2 oz. Orange Juice

Fill shaker with ingredients and shake.
Strain into tall glass filled with ice.

Andrew Thompson
Rock & Kath's Sawmill

STOLI KAFYA MARTINI

Stoli Kafya Vodka
Stoli Vanil Vodka

Serve in a chilled martini glass or over
rocks.

STOLI OH WHAT A NIGHT MARTINI

  1½ oz. Stoli Ohranj Vodka
  splash Caffe Sport Espresso Liqueur

Shake ingredients and strain into a cocktail glass. Garnish with orange slice.

STOLI POWER MARTINI

  1½ oz. Stoli Ohranj Vodka
  ½ oz. Lemon Juice
  3 oz. Orange Juice
  1 oz. Raspberry Syrup

Pour ingredients into a mixing glass, add ice, and shake well. Strain into a chilled glass and garnish with an orange peel.

STOLICHNAYA PARADISE MARTINI

  2 parts Stoli Ohranj Vodka
  1 part Orange Juice

Shake ingredients with ice. Pour into a martini glass. Garnish with an orange slice.

STRAIGHT LAW MARTINI

  1¾ oz. Dry Sherry
  ¾ oz. Dry Gin

Twist of lemon peel.

STRAWBERRY BLINTZ MARTINI

    2 oz. Stoli Strasberi Vodka
  splash Cranberry Juice

Serve shaken with a sugar-rimmed martini glass. Garnish with white chocolate dipped strawberry.

STRAWBERRY BLONDE MARTINI

    2 oz. Beefeater Gin
    1 oz. Chambraise Strawberry
            Aperitif

Twist of lemon peel.

STRAWBERRY CHOCOLATE MARTINI

  1½ oz. Strawberry Liqueur
  1½ oz. White Creme de Cacao

Shake, top with a strawberry. Serve straight up or on the rocks.

Joseph Vuckovic
Russo's on the Bay
Howard Beach, NY

STRAWBERRY MARTINI

1½ oz. Dry Gin
½ oz. Chambraise

Fresh strawberry garnish. Blend & stir.

SUPER MODEL MARTINI

2 oz. Bacardi Limón
½ oz. Melon Liqueur
½ oz. Blue Curacao
splash Martini & Rossi Extra Dry
      Vermouth

Shake ingredients with ice. Strain into chilled glasses.

STRING OF PEARLS

2½ oz. Leyden Gin
4 Cocktail Onions

Bill Chiusano
Bloomfield, NJ

SUBMARINE MARTINI

1½ oz. Dry Gin
½ oz. Dubonnet
½ oz. Dry Vermouth
1 dash Boker's Bitters

SUGAR MAGNOLIA
DARK MARTINI
  1¼ oz. Vodka
  ¾ oz. Dark Creme de Cacao
Garnish with a Hershey kiss.

SULLIVAN'S MARTINI
  3 oz. Ketel One Vodka
  ½ oz. Martini & Rossi Extra Dry
        Vermouth
        Lechee nuts
        Goachee nuts
Reebok Sports Clubs

SUMMER MARTINI
  3 oz. Gordon's Vodka
  splash Extra Dry Vermouth
  splash Cucumber Juice
Cucumber slice garnish.

SUMMERTIME MARTINI

1¼ oz. Stoli Ohranj Vodka
1¼ oz. Gordon's Grapefruit Gin
½ oz. Chambord

Shake and strain up or on the rocks.
Garnish with a flag.

Charlie's on the Lake
Omaha, NE

SUNBURST MARTINI

Orange Vodka
Dry Vermouth
Orange Slice

Yvette Wintergarden
Chicago, IL

SUNDOWNER MARTINI

2 oz. Stoli Razberi Vodka
2½ oz. Orange Juice
¼ oz. Cranberry Juice
1 or 2 splashes of Grenadine

Shake the Vodka and orange juice.
Strain into glass and add the cranberry
juice and Grenadine.

SUNFLOWER

    2 oz. Vincent Vodka
    1/2 oz. Grand Marnier
    splash Blood Orange Juice
Combine all ingredients and shake
with ice. Garnish with blood orange
wedge/edible flowers.
Andy Porter
Van Gogh's Restaurant & Bar
Atlanta, GA

SUNRISE MARTINI

    2 oz. Smirnoff Vodka
    1 oz. Cuervo 1800 Tequila
    splash Grand Marnier
    splash Grenadine
Garnish with orange slice.

SUNSET

        Stoli Ohranj Vodka
    dash Bitters
Garnished with an orange slice.

SUPER JUICE MARTINI

        Stoli Ohranj Vodka
dash Cranberry Juice
dash Orange Juice

Tunnel Bar Raphael
Providence, RI

SUPPER MARTINI

2 oz. Boodles Gin
dash Drambuie
dash Sweet Vermouth
1 Maraschino Cherry
    for garnish

Shake with ice and strain into a chilled martini glass. Garnish with maraschino cherry.

Mumbo Jumbo
Atlanta, GA

SUPREME CHOCOLATE MARTINI

        2 oz. Vodka
    1½ oz. Marie Brizard White
               Creme de Cacao
               Unsweetened Cocoa Powder
        1 Hershey's Hug Candy

Coat rim with cocoa powder and place
the kiss pointed top up in the bottom of
the glass. Stir in glass of ice until well
chilled and strain.
Marie Brizard
North Miami, FL

SURFER MARTINI

    1½ oz. Smirnoff Vodka
      ½ oz. Malibu Coconut Rum
    splash Banana Liqueur

Chill, strain and garnish with a
pineapple wedge.

SUSHI MARTINI

               Tanqueray Gin
               Martini & Rossi Extra Dry
               Vermouth

Served straight up with a Tobiko stuffed
olive and pickled Ginger.
Bruno's Club Deluxe
Chicago, IL

SWEET ARLENE

¼ oz. Apple Cider
¼ oz. Martini & Rossi Sweet
　　　 Vermouth
¼ oz. Limoncello
¼ oz. Gin
dash Bitters

Garnish with apple slice.

Steve Visakay
Vintage Cocktail Shakers

SWEET DUTCHMAN

2 parts Sweet Vermouth
1 part Leyden Gin
　　　 Orange peel

Bill Chiusano
Bloomfield, NJ

SWEET MARTINI

1½ oz. Absolut Citron Vodka
¼ oz. Extra Dry Vermouth
splash Chambord

Combine in a shaker with ice. Shake
well and strain into martini glass.
Garnish with twist of lemon.

Jane Lomshek, Bartender
Holidome
Lawrence, KS

SWISS KISS MARTINI

    2 oz. Grey Goose Vodka
    1/2 oz. Frangelico
    1/2 oz. Butterscotch Schnapps
    1 oz. Creme de Cacao
          Lace with Godet White
          Chocolate Liqueur

Sprinkle with Godiva Chocolate.

Iraklis Papachristos
Mercury Bar
Boston, MA

TAILSPIN MARTINI

    3/4 oz. Beefeater Gin
    3/4 oz. Sweet Vermouth
    3/4 oz. Green Chartreuse
  2 dashes Orange Bitters
          Olive and Lemon twist

Shake liquid ingredients with ice.
Strain into chilled glass half filled
with crushed ice. Drop in olive and
lemon twist.

TANGO COCKTAIL MARTINI

    1 oz. Gin
    ½ oz. Martini and Rossi Dry
            Vermouth
    ½ oz. Martini and Rossi Sweet
            Vermouth
    ½ oz. Fresh Orange Juice
    ½ tsp. Triple Sec

Shake ingredients with ice. Strain into chilled glass.

TAKE OFF MARTINI

        Tanqueray Gin
splash Cointreau
        Orange peel

The Windsock Bar & Grill
San Diego, CA

TANGERINE DELIGHT

        Stoli Ohranj Vodka
   dash Dark Creme de Cacao

Chill and serve up with orange twist.

Shirley Morgan, Bartender
Pier St. Pub
Jupiter, FL

TANQUERAY EXTRA DRY MARTINI

Tanqueray Gin served in chilled martini glass. Dry Vermouth. Garnish with olive.

Hurricane Restaurant
Passagrille, FL

TANQUERAY "PERFECT TEN" MARTINI

    2 oz. Tanqueray No. Ten
    1 oz. Grand Marnier
    $1/2$ oz. Sour Mix

TANQUERAY NO. TEN MARTINI

    $2^1/4$ oz. Tanqueray No. Ten
    $1^3/4$ oz. Lime Juice

Add squeeze of one lime wedge.

"AT LAST!"

TANQY BREEZY MARTINI

    3 oz. Tanqueray Gin
    dash Dry Vermouth
    1 oz. Pineapple Juice
    1 oz. Grapefruit Juice
Lemon twist or olive.
Hyman Goldfeld
Philadelphia, PA

TANTRA KISS

    3 oz. Grey Goose Vodka
    1 oz. Peach Schnapps
    splash Cranberry Juice
    splash Pineapple Juice
Shake with ice and serve straight up
with an edible pansy.
Bruce Craig
Tantra, Inc.
Miami, FL

TAPIKA'S MARTINI

    $2\frac{1}{2}$ oz. Chinaco Blanco Tequila
    $\frac{1}{2}$ oz. Cointreau
    $\frac{1}{2}$ oz. Martini & Rossi Extra Dry
              Vermouth
              Lime Wedge
Reebok Sports Clubs

TARTINI

    1½ oz. Stoli Razberi Vodka
    dash Chambord
    dash Rose's Lime Juice
    splash Cranberry Juice
Garnish with lime wedge.

TEQUILA MARTINI

Tequila, Cointreau and Grand Marnier.

TATOU'S TATOUNI

    3 oz. Ketel One Vodka
          Martini & Rossi Extra Dry
          Vermouth
    splash Cucumber Juice
Cucumbers to garnish.
Reebok Sports Clubs

TEENY WEENY CHOCOLATE MARTINI

          Ketel One Vodka
          White Creme de Cacao
Garnish with a chocolate truffle.

TEMPLE - TINI
        Absolut Kurant Vodka
sprinkle Chambord
        Maraschino Cherry

TEQUILA GIMLET MARTINI
   2 oz. Tequila
   1 oz. Lime Juice
Chill, strain and garnish with a lime
wedge.

TEQUINA MARTINI
   2 oz. Tequila
   ½ oz. Dry Vermouth
Stir Tequila and Vermouth with ice in
a mixing glass until chilled. Strain into a
chilled cocktail glass. Garnish with
lemon twist.

THAI MARTINI
Infuse Smirnoff Vodka with lemongrass
2 oz. infused Smirnoff Vodka. Chill,
strain and garnish with a fresh sprig of
coriander.

THAT'S ITALIAN MARTINI

        Ketel One Vodka
        Campari
        Orange & Lemon Slice

Yvette Wintergarden
Chicago, IL

THE "61" COSMO

Stoli Razberi Vodka shaken with cranberry juice, lime juice & Triple Sec. Garnished with raspberries & a twist.

Lot 61
New York, NY

THE ALL-AMERICAN MARTINI

  $1\frac{1}{2}$ oz. Glacier Vodka
     dash Vermouth

Garnish with two olives skewered by an American Flag toothpick.

THE "PERFECT" MARTINI

        Bombay Sapphire Gin
        Eye-dropper of Dry
        Vermouth

Garnish with jumbo shrimp and cocktail sauce.

Shulas No Name Lounge
Tampa, FL

THE "Q" MARTINI

    2 oz. Smirnoff Vodka
  splash Blue Curacao
    dash Lime Juice

Chill, strain and garnish with a lemon twist.

THE 11 ONION GIBSON

    $\frac{1}{2}$ oz. Bombay Sapphire Gin
  2 drops Dry Vermouth

Garnish with 11 cocktail onions.
Charles McMahan
New Matamoras, OH

THE GODFATHER

        Belvedere Vodka
        Grand Marnier
        Amaretto
        Martini & Rossi Extra Dry
        Vermouth

Garnish with a maraschino cherry and an orange twist.
Harry's Velvet Room
Chicago, IL

THE GRIESE MARTINI

Skyy Vodka
Godiva Liqueur

Garnish with Hershey's Kiss.
Shulas No Name Lounge
Tampa, FL

THE HOLIDAY MARTINI

1½ oz. Finlandia Cranberry Vodka
1½ oz. Absolut Kurant Vodka
½ oz. Martini & Rossi Sweet
Vermouth

Garnish with cherry.
Handshakes Bar & Grill
Hopewell Junction, NY

THE HORTON

Grey Goose Vodka
splash Orange Flower Water

THE MARK HAUSER

Ketel One Vodka
splash Chambord

The Diner on Sycamore
Cincinnati, OH

THIGH OPENER

    2 oz. O.P.

    ¼ oz. Lime Juice

    ¼ oz. Triple Sec

Shake. Serve on the rocks.

THIRD DEGREE MARTINI

Infuse Smirnoff Vodka with Jalapeño Pepper, seeds intact. Thoroughly chill Vodka in the freezer. 2 oz. Infused Smirnoff Vodka. Chill, strain and garnish with pickled yellow pepper.

THRUST MARTINI

        Hennessy V.S. Cognac

  dash Lemon Juice

        Lemon peel

The Windsock Bar & Grill

San Diego, CA

THREE CONTINENTS MARTINI
1¼ oz. Skyy Vodka
¼ oz. Grand Marnier
2 drops Blue Curacao

Shake with ice and strain into chilled
martini glass. Garnish with orange
twist.
Cliff Inn
El Paso, TX

THRILLA VANILLA MARTINI
Stoli Vanil Vodka straight up.

THUNDERER MARTINI
Stolichnaya shaken with Blue Curacao
& Cassis.
Lot 61
New York, NY

TIGER-TINI
Stolichnaya Ohranj Vodka
Grand Marnier
splash Orange Juice
The Diner on Sycamore
Cincinnati, OH

TIJUANATINI
            Ketel One Vodka
            Kahlua Liqueur
            Coffee beans

Cecilia's
Breckenridge, CO

TIO PEPE MARTINI
  7 parts Dry Gin
  2 part Tio Pepe Sherry
Twist of lemon peel.

TO RUSSIA WITH LOVE
  1½ oz. Stoli Vanil Vodka
  ½ oz. Maraschino Cherry Juice
  ½ oz. Coconut Rum
  1 oz. Cream or half & half
  1 Egg White (for two drinks)
    Maraschino Cherry

Mix all ingredients, except maraschino cherry, with cracked ice in a shaker or blender and strain into a chilled cocktail glass. Garnish with maraschino cherry.

TOASTED ALMOND MARTINI

2½ oz. Stoli Vanil Vodka
½ oz. Stoli Kafya Vodka
1 splash Amaretto

Garnish with almond or hazelnut.

TONIGHT OR NEVER MARTINI

1 oz. Dry Gin
1 oz. Dry Vermouth
½ oz. Cognac

TOPAZ MARTINI

1¾ oz. Bacardi Limón
¼ oz. Martini & Rossi Extra Dry
Vermouth
splash Blue Curacao

Combine in a cocktail glass.

TOPAZ MARTINI II

5 parts Gordon's Vodka
1 part Dark Creme de Cacao
1 part Frangelico

Float 3 whole roasted coffee beans in glass.

TRES MARTINI

1½ oz. Sauza Tres Generaciones
Tequila
splash Cointreau

Rinse a chilled martini glass with a splash of Cointreau and discard. Place Tres Generaciones in a shaker. Fill with ice, shake and strain into the prepared glass. Garnish with Orange Zest.

TRILBY MARTINI

1¼ oz. Dry Gin
1 oz. Sweet Vermouth
2 dashes Orange Bitters

Stir. Float ¼ oz. Creme de Yvette on the surface or Chambord.

TRINITY MARTINI aka TRIO PLAZA MARTINI

1 oz. Bombay Gin
1 oz. half Rosso Vermouth and half
Extra Dry Vermouth

Stir in cocktail glass. Strain & serve straight up or on the rocks. Add lemon twist or olives.

TRIPLE G MARTINI

    2 oz. Grey Goose Vodka
    dash Hershey's Syrup in glass
    1 oz. Godet or White Chocolate
          Liqueur

Shake gently. Garnish with Hershey's
Syrup.

Erica Frene of The Rack
Boston, MA

TROPICAL MARTINI

   1½ oz. Smirnoff Vodka
  splash Malibu Rum
  splash Pineapple Juice

Chill, strain and garnish with
Pineapple.

TROPICAL MARTINI II

    2 oz. Malibu or Parrot Bay
          Coconut Rum
    ½ oz. Pineapple Juice
  splash Rose's Lime Juice
    dash Salt

Shake, add ice, shake again, and strain
into chilled martini glass. Garnish with
whatever fruit is available.

Amanda
E-mail

TROPICAL MARTINI III

Stoli Ohranj, Stoli Vanil Vodkas and
Pineapple Juice.
Renaissance Atlanta Hotel
Atlanta, GA

TROPICAL SPELLBINDER

Absolut Citron Vodka
Blue Curacao
Midori

TROPITINI MARTINI

Finlandia Vodka
Bacardi Limón
Blue Curacao
Pineapple Juice
whisper Martini & Rossi Extra Dry
Vermouth

Shaken, strained and garnish with
pineapple.
Martini Ranch
Chicago, IL

TRUFFLE

> Absolut Kurant Vodka
> Creme de Cacao

Portland's Best
Portland, OR

TULIP COCKTAIL

3/4 oz. Apple Brandy
3/4 oz. Sweet Vermouth
2 tsp. Apricot Brandy
1 1/2 tsp. Fresh Lemon Juice

Shake ingredients with cracked ice.
Strain into chilled glass.

TURANTINI

1 1/2 oz. Turantula Tequila
1/4 oz. Cointreau
splash Rose's Lime Juice

Garnish with lime twist.

Tim Parsons
Pegasus
San Antonio, TX

TUXEDO MARTINI

$1\frac{1}{4}$ oz. Dry Gin
$1\frac{1}{4}$ oz. Dry Vermouth
$\frac{1}{4}$ oz. Maraschino Cherry Juice
$\frac{1}{4}$ tsp. Pernod
2 dashes Orange Bitters
Twist of lemon peel.

TWISTED BREEZE MARTINI

$1\frac{1}{2}$ oz. Smirnoff Citrus Twist Vodka
dash Grapefruit Juice
dash Cranberry Juice
Chill, strain and serve with fresh cranberries.

TWISTED CITRUS MARTINI

2 oz. frozen Smirnoff Citrus Twist Vodka. Chill, strain and garnish with large wedges of lemon and lime squeezed into the Vodka.

"THIS IS ALL THE SOCIAL
SECURITY I NEED,
A VODKA MARTINI!"

TWISTED HOUND MARTINI

    1 oz. Smirnoff Vodka
  splash Freshly squeezed Pink
           Grapefruit Juice

Chill and strain into well chilled martini glass.

TWISTED PLAZA MARTINI

  1½ oz. Smirnoff Citrus Twist Vodka
    dash Melon Liqueur
  splash Pineapple Juice and
           Orange Juice

Chill, strain and garnish with a fresh pineapple wedge.

TWISTED-TINI

        Smirnoff Citrus Twist Vodka
        Dry Vermouth

Shaken, not stirred.

Martini's
New York, NY

390

TWISTING KURANT

    2 oz. Absolut Kurant Vodka
        Big splash Sweet Vermouth
Strain into chilled martini glass. Serve
with sugar coated lemon twist.
Olive Garden
Lincoln, NE

TWO LIPS MARTINI

        Leyden Gin
    splash Chambord
Bill Chiusano
Bloomfield, NJ

TYNE'S MARTINI

    3 shots Vodka
     twist Lemon
Shake gently with ice. Dash of Captain
Morgan Spiced Rum.
Tyne Caouette
Portage, MI

U.S.A. MARTINI

Teton Glacier Vodka (made in the
U.S.A.) Splash of Vermouth.

ULTIMATE CHILL

$2\frac{1}{2}$ oz. Bombay Sapphire Gin or
         Stolichnaya Gold Vodka
$\frac{1}{4}$ oz. Cinzano Dry Vermouth

Garnished with 2 large Vermouth-
marinated Italian olives.

Marcus Nates & Steve Burney
Oliver's in the Mayflower Park Hotel
Seattle, WA

ULTIMATE MARTINI

1 oz. Stoli Vodka
$\frac{1}{2}$ oz. Campari
$\frac{1}{4}$ oz. Sweet Vermouth

ULTIMATE MARTINI II

         Boodles British Dry Gin
         Whisper of Dry Vermouth
         Queen Olives Stuffed with
         Stilton Cheese

Polo Lounge
Windsor Court Hotel
New Orleans, LA

UNDER THE VOLCANO MARTINI

The Encantado Martini – 100 % Mezcal with Martini & Rossi Vermouth. Garnish with a Jalapeño stuffed olive.

UNION LEAGUE MARTINI

1¾ oz. Old Tom Gin
¾ oz. Port Wine
1 dash Orange Bitters

UP UP & AWAY

Beefeater Gin
splash Grapefruit Juice
Lemon twist

The Windsock Bar & Grill
San Diego, CA

UPTOWN ALIZÉ

2 oz. Hennessy
2 oz. Alizé Red Passion
Serve over ice.

Sidney Masters
The Shark Bar
New York, NY

USABAY MARTINI

   1¾ oz. Vodka
   ½ oz. Captain Morgan Parrot Bay
           Coconut Rum
Garnish with coconut twist.
Chris Hammond
The Thirsty Turtle
Bernardsville, NJ

USA, PRINCE OF MARTINI

   ¾ oz. Vodka
   ½ oz. Wild Spirit
   dash Vermouth
Garnish with orange wheel.
Steve Prince
The Thirsty Turtle
Bernardsville, NJ

VALERIE

       Tanqueray Gin
  splash Olive Juice
Top with 2 olives.
Wendy Michaels
Branding Iron
Yamhill, OR

VAMPIRE MARTINI

    2 oz. Stolichnaya Vodka
    ½ oz. Chambord
    touch Cranberry Juice

No. 18
New York, NY

VAMPIRE MARTINI II

    1 oz. Beefeater Gin
    1 oz. Martini and Rossi Dry
           Vermouth
    ½ oz. Lime Juice

Shake.

VAN MARTINI

    1¾ oz. Dry Gin
    ½ oz. Dry Vermouth
    ¼ oz. Grand Marnier

VANILLA BEANI

    1 oz. Stoli Vanil Vodka
    splash Tuaca

Garnish with vanilla bean.

Peggy Howell
Cotati Yacht Club & Saloon
Cotati, CA

VANILLA MARTINI

Freshly muddled vanilla beans shaken
with Belvedere Vodka & sugar.

Lot 61
New York, NY

VANILLA RAIN

    1 part Rain Vodka chilled
    1 part Dr. Vanillacuddy chilled
Strain into martini glass.

VEGGIE MARTINI

    2½ oz. Tanqueray Gin
Garnish with green and black olives,
onions and baby carrots.

Cecilia's
Breckenridge, CO

VELOCITY MARTINI

    1½ oz. Bombay Gin
      dash Martini & Rossi Extra Dry
            Vermouth
Add orange slice. Shake, strain & serve
up or on the rocks with some ice.

VELOUR MARTINI

   1½ oz. Smirnoff Vodka
   splash Blue Curacao
   splash Cranberry Juice
Chill, strain and garnish with
cranberries.

VELVET BUNNY MARTINI

Combine 1½ oz. Smirnoff Vodka with
Dash of Banana Liqueur and Romana
Black Sambuca. Strain and garnish with
banana slice.

VELVET CITRUS MARTINI

   2½ oz. Gordon's Citrus Vodka
          Lemon twist.

VELVETINI

   3 oz. Grey Goose Vodka
   ½ oz. Poires D'Anjou
   dash DiSaronno Amaretto
   dash Godiva Dark Chocolate
          Liqueur
Shake hard with ice. Strain into chilled
martini glass. Garnish with one strawberry.
Brady and Dina Martin
Hudson Club
Chicago, IL

VENDOME MARTINI

    1 oz. Beefeater Gin
    1 oz. Dubonnet
    ½ oz. Dry Vermouth
Twist of lemon peel.

VERMOUTH CASSIS MARTINI

  2 parts Martini & Rossi Dry
             Vermouth
   1 part Creme de Cassis
Pour over ice and stir well.

VERMOUTH COCKTAIL MARTINI

    1 oz. Dry Vermouth
    1 oz. Sweet Vermouth
 2 dashes Orange Bitters
             Maraschino Cherry
Stir liquid ingredients with ice. Strain
into chilled glass. Garnish with
maraschino cherry.

VERMOUTH RINSE MARTINI

Coat the inside of a glass with Dry
Vermouth. Shake off the excess. Fill the
glass with chilled Beefeater Gin. Add a
twist of lemon peel or green olive.

VERMOUTH TRIPLE SEC MARTINI

    1 oz. Martini and Rossi Dry Vermouth
    1 oz. Dry Gin
    ½ oz. Triple Sec
2 dashes Orange Bitters
Twist of lemon peel.

VERY BERRY MARTINI

    2 oz. Gin
    ½ oz. Cranberry Juice Cocktail
Combine in ice filled shaker. Shake and strain into well chilled martini glass. Garnish with fresh berry of your choice.
Brigid Heckman
Rexville, NY

VERY DRY MARTINI

    5 parts Beefeater Gin
    1 part French Vermouth
Twist of lemon peel.

VESPERS

    2 parts Ketel One Vodka
    1 part Tanqueray Gin
    splash Lillet

Lloyd Heslip
E-mail

VICTOR MARTINI

    1½ oz. Dry Vermouth
    ½ oz. Dry Gin
    ½ oz. Brandy

VIKING

    2½ oz. Absolut Kurant Vodka
    ½ oz. Chambord

Garnish twist.

VIKING SERUM MARTINI

    3 parts Classic Finlandia Vodka
    3 parts Seltzer
    splash Blue Curacao
    splash Cranberry Juice

VIOLETTA

   2½ oz. Absolut Vodka
   ½ oz. Blue Curacao
  splash Cranberry Juice
Garnish with a twist.

V.I.P. MARTINI

Fill a stemmed cocktail glass
with chilled Dry Gin. Waft a
fine spray of Dry Vermouth gently
on the surface from an atomizer.
Add a twist of lemon peel or a
green olive.

VISAMINI

   1 oz. Absolut Kurant Vodka
   1 oz. Bacardi Limón
   ¼ oz. Midori
  dash Rose's Lime Juice
Steve Visakay
Vintage Cocktail Shakers

**VODKA GIBSON
MARTINI**

Premium Vodka
dash Vermouth

Shaken or stirred. Garnish with an
onion, or two or three.

VODKA MARTINI

2 oz. Vodka
$\frac{1}{2}$ oz. Dry Vermouth

Twist of lemon peel or green olive.

VOODOO MARTINI

Chill 2 oz. Smirnoff Vodka in shaker.
Thinly slice clove of garlic and place at
bottom of the martini glass. Strain
Vodka into glass. Top with pepper.
Garnish with lemon wedge.

VUK'S MARTINI

$1\frac{1}{2}$ oz. Baileys Irish Cream
$1\frac{1}{2}$ oz. White Creme de Cacao

Shake, and serve straight up or on the rocks. The best way to have this martini is with ice cream. Put all ingredients in a blender and whip it up.

Joseph Vuckovic
Russo's on the Bay
Howard Beach, NY

WAI LIN MARTINI

2 oz. Smirnoff Vodka
$\frac{1}{4}$ oz. Cranberry Juice
$\frac{1}{4}$ oz. Melon Liqueur

Strain and garnish with lemon.

WAITING FOR GODET MARTINI

2 oz. Smirnoff Vodka
dash Godet Belgium White
Chocolate Liqueur
dash Bourbon

Chill, strain and garnish with a fresh strawberry.

WALLET CHAIN

    2 oz. Stoli Pertsovka or Absolut
             Peppar Vodka
    dash Worcestershire Sauce
  splash Jalepeño Stuffed olive juice
Garnish with jalepeño olives and pearl
onions.

Jim Stacy
The Manhattan Café
Athens, GA

WALLICK MARTINI

  1½ oz. Bombay Gin
    dash Martini & Rossi Extra Dry
           Vermouth
Add dash of Hiram Walker Orange
Curacao. Stir in cocktail glass. Strain &
serve straight up or on the rocks. Add
lemon twist or olives.

WALTER MARTINI

   5 parts Dry Gin
  ½ part Dry Vermouth
  ½ part Dry Sherry
 2 drops Lemon Juice

"TO LIFE... LIBERTY...AND TO THE
PURSUIT OF THREE MORE MARTINIS."

WARDEN MARTINI

    1$\frac{1}{2}$ oz. Bombay Gin
    dash Martini & Rossi Extra Dry
            Vermouth
    dash Pernod

Stir in cocktail glass. Strain & serve
straight up or on the rocks. Add lemon
twist or olives.

WATERMELON MARTINI

    2 oz. Absolut Citron Vodka
  splash Rose's Lime Juice
    4 oz. Watermelon Juice

Pour over ice and shake vigorously.
Strain into chilled 4 oz. martini glasses.

WATERMELON MARTINI II

    5 oz. Grey Goose Vodka
  $\frac{1}{2}$ oz. Cranberry Juice
  $\frac{1}{2}$ oz. Sour Mix

WAYNE'S MARTINI

    3 oz. Beefeater Gin
    $\frac{1}{8}$ oz. Glen Ord Single Malt Scotch

Stir gently over cracked ice. Strain into chilled 5 oz. martini glass. Garnish with 2 green olives stuffed with anchovy.

Wayne Beckwith
Fairport Village Inn
Fairport, NY

WELL WHAT THE PEOPLE THINK ARE MARTINIS!

    1 oz. Absolut Vodka
    1 oz. Bombay Gin
    $\frac{5}{8}$ oz. Fresh Squeezed Lemon Juice
    $1\frac{1}{4}$ oz. Grand Marnier
    1 oz. Cranberry Juice

Chill in shaker and serve up in prechilled martini glass. Garnish with $\frac{1}{4}$ inch lemon wheel caramelized with sugar.

Daryle Norberg, Bartender
Byron's Sports Bar
San Leandro, CA

WEMBLEY MARTINI

   1½ oz. Dry Gin
   ¾ oz. Dry Vermouth
   ¼ oz. Apple Brandy
  1 dash Apricot-Flavored Brandy

WEST PEACHTREE MARTINI

      Stolichnaya Persik Vodka
Flavor with dash of cranberry juice.
Renaissance Atlanta Hotel
Atlanta, GA

WHITE CHOCOLATE MARTINI

   1½ oz. Skyy Vodka
   ½ oz. Godiva Chocolate Liqueur
Chill glass, rim with chocolate shell.
Shake ingredients and pour into chilled,
rimmed glass. Garnish with a "Hershey
Hugs Kiss."
Pamela Conaway
Hurricane Restaurant
Passagrille, FL

WHITE LADY

   ³/₄ oz. Cointreau
1½ oz. Gin
   ⅓ oz. Lemon Juice
Shake with ice. Strain into a martini glass.
Remy Amerique, Inc.
New York, NY

WHITE RUSSIAN MARTINI

2 oz. Smirnoff Vodka
1 oz. Kahlua
1 oz. Half and Half
Strain into chilled martini glass.

WHITE WAY COCKTAIL MARTINI

1½ oz. Beefeater Gin
   ³/₄ oz. White Creme de Menthe
Shake ingredients with cracked ice.
Strain into chilled glass.

WHY NOT MARTINI

1 oz. Beefeater Gin
1 oz. Apricot Brandy
1 tsp. Lemon Juice
Chill, strain and serve with a lemon twist.

WILD HORSE

    1½ oz. Stoli Razberi Vodka
    ½ oz. Amaretto

Serve chilled in martini glass. Garnish
with fresh raspberry.

Iris Vourlatos
E-mail

WILD ROSE MARTINI

    1½ oz. Dry Gin
    ½ oz. Dry Vermouth
    ½ oz. Sweet Vermouth
    1 dash Orange Bitters
    1 dash Angostura Bitters

WILL ROGERS MARTINI

    1½ oz. Gin
    ½ oz. Dry Vermouth
    ½ oz. Orange Juice
    1½ tsp. Triple Sec

Shake ingredients with ice. Strain into
chilled glass.

WILSON SPECIAL MARTINI

    2 oz. Dry Gin
    ¼ oz. Dry Vermouth
    2 Orange Slices

Shake.

WINDEX MARTINI

    1 oz. Ketel One Vodka
   1/2 oz. Cointreau
    1 oz. Sour Mix
    1 oz. 7-Up

Rim glass with lemon and sugar. Shake well and add maraschino cherry.

Lisa McArthur
Cheerleaders
Philadelphia, PA

WINDEX MARTINI II

Glass filled with ice

  2 1/2 oz. Vodka
   1/2 oz. Blue Curacao
    2 oz. Lemonade

Shake and serve with strainer and martini glass.

WINDSOCK MARTINI

          Absolut Kurant Vodka
splash Cranberry Juice
          Lemon Juice
          Lemon peel

The Windsock Bar & Grill
San Diego, CA

XANTHIA MARTINI
1½ oz. Dry Gin
1 oz. Dry Vermouth
1 oz. Cointreau
Mix and serve on the rocks.

YACHTING CLUB MARTINI
1¾ oz. Holland's Gin
¾ oz. Dry Vermouth
2 dashes Peychaud's Bitters
1 dash Pernod
Sweeten with sugar to taste.

YACHTING MARTINI
1½ oz. Smirnoff Vodka
splash Peach Schnapps
splash Melon Liqueur
Chill, strain and garnish with a fresh peach wedge.

YALE COCKTAIL MARTINI
1½ oz. Beefeater Gin
½ oz. Dry Vermouth
1 tsp. Blue Curacao
dash Bitters
Stir.

YALE MARTINI

   1²/₃ oz. Plymouth Gin
    ¹/₂ oz. Dry Vermouth
2 dashes Orange Bitters
    ¹/₄ oz. Maraschino Cherry Juice
Sweeten with sugar to taste.

YANG MARTINI

  2¹/₂ oz. Gin
    ¹/₂ oz. Sake
Stir with ice and strain into a chilled
martini glass.
Inagiku
New York, NY

YELLOW DAISY

  1¹/₂ oz. Beefeater Gin
    ¹/₂ oz. Dry Vermouth
    ¹/₄ oz. Grand Marnier
    ¹/₄ oz. Pernod
          Maraschino Cherry

YELLOW FINGERS MARTINI

1½ oz. Gin
¾ oz. Blackberry Brandy
½ oz. Creme de Banana
½ oz. Cream

Shake ingredients with ice. Strain into chilled glass.

YELLOW RATTLER

2 oz. Bombay Sapphire Gin
1 oz. Extra Dry Vermouth
1 dash Orange Bitters
2 Cocktail Onions

YING MARTINI

2½ oz. Sake
½ oz. Gin

Stir with ice and strain into a chilled martini glass.

Inagiku
New York, NY

YOLANDA MARTINI

¾ oz. Dry Gin
¾ oz. Brandy
½ oz. Sweet Vermouth
¼ oz. Grenadine
¼ oz. Pernod

YORK MARTINI

  7 parts Dry Gin
    1 part French Vermouth
  1 drop Scotch
Twist of lemon peel.

YUKON MARTINI

  2 oz. Smirnoff Vodka
  dash Yukon Jack to coat the
         martini glass
Chill and strain Vodka into the coated
martini glass. Garnish with a lemon
wedge.

YVETTE MARTINI

      Ketel One Vodka
      Grand Marnier
      Garnish with an orange twist.
Yvette Wintergarden
Chicago, IL

ZANZIBAR MARTINI

2½ oz. Dry Vermouth
1 oz. Gin
½ oz. Lemon Juice
1 tsp. Sugar Syrup
3 dashes Bitters

Chill, strain and garnish with a lemon twist.

ZARA MARTINI

1¾ oz. Old Tom Gin
¾ oz. Dubonnet
1 dash Orange Bitters

ZINAMARTINI

1½ oz. Stoli Zinamon Vodka
¼ oz. Dry Vermouth

Pour Vermouth into glass. Discard Vermouth and add Stoli. Garnish with cinnamon stick. Serve in martini glass.

Joe Chironno
Celebrity Pub
Wheatley Heights, NY

ZINAMON TOAST MARTINI

2 oz. Stoli Zinamon Vodka
1/2 oz. Cinnamon Schnapps

Serve in chilled martini glass. Garnish with cinnamon stick.

Debbie Wolklewicz
The Big Chill
Chattanooga, TN

ZORBATINI MARTINI

1 1/2 oz. Stolichnaya Vodka
1/4 oz. Metaxa Ouzo

Stir gently with ice and strain. Garnish with a green olive.

"007" MARTINI

Rinse glass with extra dry Vermouth

1 oz. Gordon's Vodka
1 oz. Gordon's Gin
1/2 oz. Lillet Blanc

Lemon twist garnish.

---

151 MARTINI BACARDI

Bacardi 151 Rum
Martini & Rossi Rosso
Vermouth

Shake and strain into a martini glass. Splash of cranberry juice. Garnish with a twist.

1800 CARATS MARTINI

> Cuervo 1800 Tequila
> Grand Marnier
> Lime squeeze

Gatsby
Boca Raton, FL

1940's CLASSIC MARTINI

> Tanqueray
> Noilly Prat Dry Vermouth

Garnish with an olive.
Continental Café
Philadelphia, PA

1951 MARTINI

> 2 oz. Gordon's Gin
> splash Cointreau
> Anchovy Stuffed Olive

Rinse glass with Cointreau. Add the Gin and olive.

24-KARROT MARTINI

Ketel One with a spicy baby carrot.
Straight up or over ice.

THE BEST OF

THE ULTIMATE COCKTAIL BOOK II
- Contains signature drinks from America's top bars
- Drinks (categorized) by name and product
- Complete beer section
- History of today's cocktails and their origins
- Over 1,300 recipes
- Only $12.95 (includes shipping & handling)

SPIRITED CHEF – Featuring America's Finest Chefs
- Over 100 recipes cooking with spirits
- Featuring recipes from America's best chefs and favorite Liquor and Brewing Companies
- Cook with your favorite liquor
- Food and drink lovers' favorites
- From appetizers to desserts
- Color photos
- $20.00 (includes shipping & handling)

THE ULTIMATE LITTLE BOOKS WITH BIG RECIPES

THE ULTIMATE LITTLE SHOOTER BOOK
- Over 1,000 shooter recipes
- A must have book
- Every shooter imaginable-plus
- For the professional bartender
- History of the shot
- $10.95 (includes shipping & handling)

THE ULTIMATE LITTLE BLENDER BOOK
- Over 1,000 frozen drinks
- Non-alcoholic recipes
- Tips on blenders
- Classic as well as new recipes
- $10.95 (includes shipping & handling)

CALL 1-800-46-DRINK (1-800-463-7465) NOW TO PLACE YOUR CREDIT CARD ORDER OR

B A R   B O O K S

Special offer from *BARTENDER* Magazine

The Art of LeRoy Neiman

Dublin Bar
"The Stags Head"
22 7/8" x 33 1/4",
15 colors

F.X. McRory's Whiskey Bar — Seattle
22 1/8" x 38"

Polo Lounge
17 3/4" x 39 1/2'

La Grande Cuisine
23" x 25 3/4"

Mark McGwire, 36" x 24" vertical.
The print pays tribute to
Mark McGwire of the St. Louis
Cardinals, who hit 70 home
runs in the 1998 baseball
season shattering the previous
record of 60. In 1999, he hit 65,
again winning the home run
championship.

BARTENDER Magazine's
Specialty Products

100% cotton and water-resistant with
low profile crown. Adjustable self-fabric
strap with brass-tone buckle, snap
fastener and grommet hide-away.
$15.00 (plus $2.00 shipping.)

Bartender Zippo Lighter
$25.00 (includes shipping)

The one and only
"BEARTENDER"
(11" tall) $20.00
(includes shipping)

Bar Signals Poster
23" x 29", $15.00
(plus $5 shipping)

Credit card orders phone: 1-800-46-DRINK
(9:00am – 9:00pm M-F, EST only) Or send
check or money order to: BARTENDER,
PO Box 158, Liberty Corner, NJ 07938-9986,
www.bartender.com or barmag@aol.com

We accept the
following cards: